{Hartford}

New England Renaissance

Hartford {*New England Renaissance*}

INTRODUCTION BY Bob Steele

ART DIRECTION BY Enrique Espinosa

URBAN
TAPESTRY
SERIES
TOWERY
PUBLISHING, INC.

Contents

By Bob Steele

SOME CITIES ARE KNOWN AS COMPANY TOWNS. Hartford is more than that. It's an industry town. And the industry, of course, is insurance. It was true back in 1936, when I moved here from Los Angeles to serve as an announcer on WTIC Radio, and it is true today. Even my employer's call letters reflected the dominance of this one industry—the station was then owned, you see, by the Travelers Insurance Companies.

In the 60-plus years that I have worked in radio in Hartford, many things have changed. But not the bedrock influence of the city's huge, internationally prominent insurance companies. While this is widely known about the community, few people are aware of just why Hartford has long been known as the Insurance Capital of the World.

The reason has to do with pirates. And shipwrecks. And hurricanes. From its founding in the 1630s, Hartford's position on the Connecticut River—just 38 miles from Long Island Sound—has been one of its main assets, making it a shipping hub for many of New England's towns and villages. Boston, Providence, New York—all were shipping hubs, of course, larger and more active than Hartford in the grand scheme. But Hartford's inland location gave farmers easier access to vessels transporting the stuff—crops, seeds, supplies, livestock, and the like— that they needed to live. They didn't want to have to travel for several days to buy what they needed, and then haul it back home, when they could have the same commodities delivered right to their front doors.

Nor did local farmers want to take a chance on losing a year or two of income due to a shipping mishap. A fire on board a ship was a disaster, along with the aforementioned shipwrecks, hurricanes, pirates, icebergs, and myriad other calamities. So, way back in 1810, when the insurance ☞

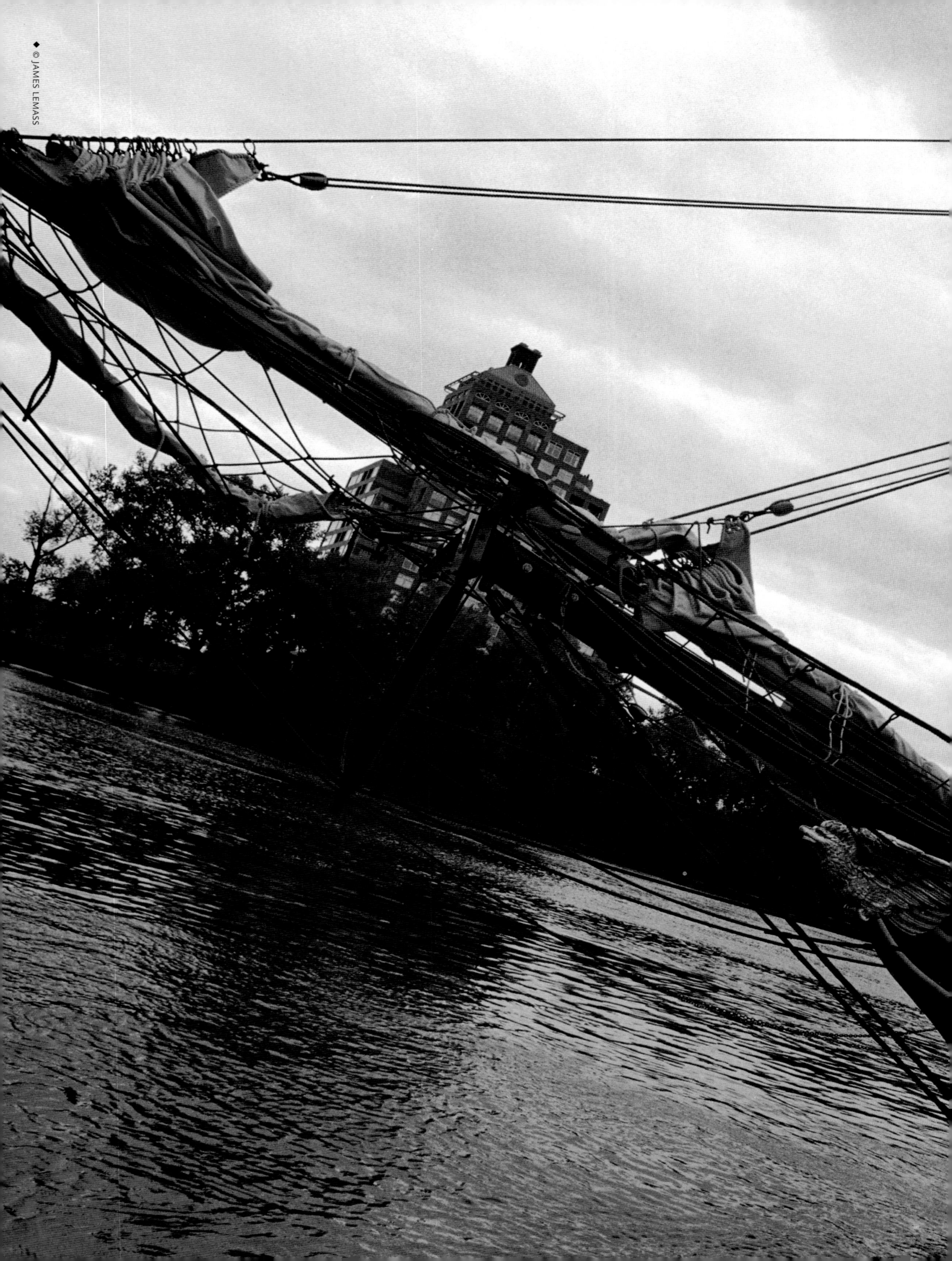

◆ © JAMES LEMASS

industry was just being born in England, some farsighted businessmen who had been taking risks decided to enter into a more formal arrangement to protect their investments. They formed an organization that is still in business as the Hartford Insurance Group, the oldest insurance company in the country that's still in operation. Soon, the firm was joined by others, and Hartford emerged as home to such giants as Aetna and Travelers.

While insurance is what the city of Hartford is known for in business circles, people are often surprised to learn how diversified the local economy is. Manufacturing once thrived here (Hartford was the home for Samuel Colt's firearms company), and remains a significant segment of

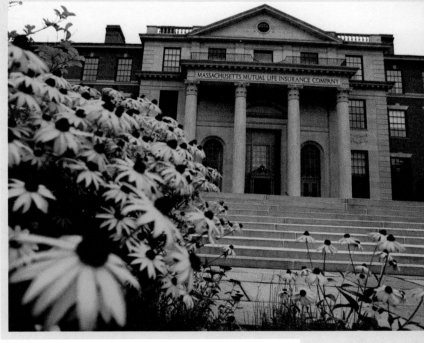

the local economy. Real estate and finance are also big in Hartford, as are technology and service industries. Two brands of world-famous typewriters—Underwood and Royal— were manufactured in Hartford, as were Pope automobiles, motorcycles, and bicycles. Pratt & Whitney aircraft engines are also built here.

To fully understand the area's economic diversity, it helps to realize that what most people think of as the city of Hartford is also an entire constellation of communities. Known by most as Greater Hartford, this group includes more than 30 villages and towns in the central Connecticut valley. Here, in these villages, is a wealth of cultural and social diversity, not to mention practically every kind of business under the sun. Traditional manufacturing, high-tech companies, service industries—they all thrive here.

It would be impossible to list all of the communities that make up Greater Hartford. There's just too much going on to do justice to them. But even the names of many of these communities will resonate with folks who barely know the place. Towns like Andover, Avon, Bloomfield, Coventry, East Hartford and West Hartford, Enfield, Farmington, Glastonbury, ☞

Granby, Manchester, New Britain, Rocky Hill, Wethersfield, and Windsor (and East Windsor and South Windsor)—all contribute to the area's fascinating mix. Whether they are known primarily as residential communities, or as places of historical significance, or merely for their New England beauty, these communities join to form what most people commonly refer to as Hartford. Locals identify both with their smaller community and with Greater Hartford. Nobody around here seems to get upset or confused by it, and newcomers quickly learn the program.

The most obvious change to Hartford, since I arrived more than 60 years ago, is the cityscape. The buildings that have gone up are numerous and enormous. There are the skyscrapers—the 30- and 40-story buildings—that replaced the rows of brownstone office buildings that once made up the downtown business district. Particularly noteworthy is the Phoenix Mutual Building, shaped like an enormous boat—a real eye-opener because it's one of the few two-sided buildings in the country. And, of course, they've improved the highways that get the people in from the suburbs—greatly. We still have lots of traffic congestion, but if it weren't for these highways,

nobody would ever get to work or get home. There's been a lot more new construction—the Civic Center, for instance—but the change that still strikes me is how much Hartford now resembles a big city, with all the big buildings and all the hustle and traffic.

In the face of all this building, a lot of old landmarks are gone, of course. Downtown's Asylum Street and Main Street were once the center for stores with well-known names that no longer exist. Places like G. Fox, which was the biggest and most famous, were there. The store was established in 1847, and was the biggest in this area. The building stands vacant now. Or Horsfall's, a men's store. Or big department stores like ☞

Wise Smith, Sage-Allen, and Brown Thompson. I recall doing a lot of window shopping down there. Leopold Morse, for instance, used to sell French Shriner and Urner shoes—the best—and they used to put them in the window. They sold for $12.95 a pair, which was more than I could afford, so I used to just stare at them when I'd pass by. Some of the stores are still thriving. The exclusive, high-priced, and high-quality Stackpole, Moore, Tryon—people call it Stack's—is going strong. And we do have a mall now that has big stores in it, like Lord & Taylor, Filene's, and Nordstrom—but they didn't exist when I came to town.

Today, Asylum is just a street. It's got stores, sure, but the excitement of going to the big department stores and just looking around is gone.

It wasn't just the shopping that made the district exciting, though. There were big theaters—most on Main, but a couple on Asylum—as well. The State Theater brought nationally known entertainers every week and seated about 3,000 people. There were the Strand Theater, the Loew's Palace, the Loew's Poli, the E.M. Loew's, the Princess, and the Allyn. They don't exist any more. They're out of business, replaced by all the multiscreen movie theaters at the malls and in the suburbs.

And then there were places like the Allyn House, an old and famous hotel that no longer exists. It was razed, and they built the Civic Center on that spot. Other hotels on Asylum Street were the Bond and the Garde, now just memories.

What's gratifying to me, though, is the way that Hartford knows when to let well enough alone and preserve its past. You hear the quote all the time from Mark Twain, who lived here from 1874 to 1891, about how "of all the beautiful towns it has been my fortune to see, this is the chief." ☞

Twain wasn't the only author to find a home here. Harriet Beecher Stowe also made her home here, as did Wallace Stevens, who worked days in the insurance business and went home at night to craft his wonderful poetry.

Preservation is only part of the story, though. There is progress as well. New developments replace the old, and somehow the balance between what used to be and what will be creates a tremendously positive environment. Today, there are big plans for a revival of the downtown area, including a retail and entertainment section called Adriaen's Landing among the many ideas for carrying Hartford's wonderful legacy forward.

And yet, Hartford is an old city, and you're reminded of it throughout the area. The *Hartford Courant*, which dates back to 1764, is the oldest paper in the country that's still in continuous publication. The Wadsworth Atheneum Museum of Art, which opened in 1842, is the country's oldest public art museum. It received a prominent vote of support (and funding) from J.P. Morgan, who came from Hartford. The Wadsworth Atheneum is still one of the top art museums in the country, and a wonderful place to visit.

Another historical site is the Connecticut capitol, made out of marble and granite. The building was opened in 1879, and houses a good many objects of historical interest. But the real architectural treasure is the Old State House, one of Charles Bulfinch's most definitive colonial designs. The Old State House dates back to 1796, making it the oldest in the United States. I'm sure that George Washington and Abraham Lincoln have both been there. It's now a cultural center—right in the middle of downtown Hartford—facing the river, undiminished by all the tall buildings that soar above it. ☞

The big cultural hub for the fine arts and movies is Bushnell Memorial Hall—famous for its architecture, and still going strong after many, many years (it was opened in 1928). Bushnell Memorial Hall is just a beautiful building, undergoing big-time renovation, which will help preserve it for future generations. Today, the hall is home to the symphony orchestra, the ballet company, the opera, and a several other performing arts groups.

Everywhere you go, in Hartford or in the communities that make up the region, you realize that this is a place of real history. It's so old, but it's also important for a lot of things that helped make the country into what it is today. People respect that, and they want to save what's best about

what used to be. Historical homes and museums dot the area and are too numerous to even try to mention. The result, though, is that there's a great blend of the past and the present here that keeps the area an exciting place to live.

Of course, there are plenty of other ways to have fun that aren't necessarily tied to history. I've always enjoyed going to the big amusement parks. One—actually in Massachusetts about 20 miles from us—is Riverside Park, where everybody goes to ride the giant roller coaster and experience other hair-raising excursions. Another is Lake Compounce in Bristol. Both are pretty old, but both are still going strong.

There are plenty of parks. Foremost among them is certainly Bushnell Park, which was designed by Hartford native Frederick Law Olmsted, the man responsible for New York's Central Park. In addition to its acres of beautiful natural areas, Bushnell Park has a famous Civil War memorial, the Soldiers and Sailors Memorial Arch, as well as the terrific old Stein and Goldstein carousel, which first spun its magic in 1914. Other parks in the Hartford area include the McLean Game Refuge, Talcott Mountain ☞

State Park, and Dinosaur State Park, to name just a few that feature every kind of outdoor activity you might want. The Elizabeth Park Rose Gardens is one of the best places in town to take a summer stroll; it's the oldest municipal rose garden in the country, and the people who run it obviously are aware of its prominence.

Sports fans in the community can follow the Hartford Wolf Pack hockey team of the AHL, or the University of Connecticut basketball Huskies, or any of the Boston and New York teams. And golf fans rejoice each year when the famous Hartford Open is played in nearby Cromwell.

Back when I began my career as a broadcaster, radio was pretty well established, but it was just entering its glory days, its maturity. Radio broadcasting had been in Hartford for about 15 years, and everybody listened to the radio, or went to the movies for entertainment—since there was no television, of course.

But for a lot of people, just listening to the radio was not enough. Lots of people would come to the big stations like ours at WTIC and crowd into theaterlike areas where they could watch the announcer or news reporter, just to see him and hear him speaking at the same time. It was a big deal. Also, WTIC had live drama, and musical concerts with fine orchestras comprised of top area musicians and conductors. It was all live, and there was this real interest among people in coming into the studio and seeing how it all worked.

You could say that Hartford has this same sort of appeal. It's a city that's so fascinating, with so much history and natural beauty and activity, that it serves as a never-ending lure for those who are curious to come and see what the magic is all about. ❁

H ARTFORD'S SKYLINE WELCOMES residents and visitors by showing off the architectural master-pieces that define its character (PAGES 34-39). Magnificent structures such as the Travelers Tower (PAGE 36)—the headquarters for Travelers Insurance—and Horace Bushnell Memorial Hall (PAGES 38 AND 39) dominate the city's core.

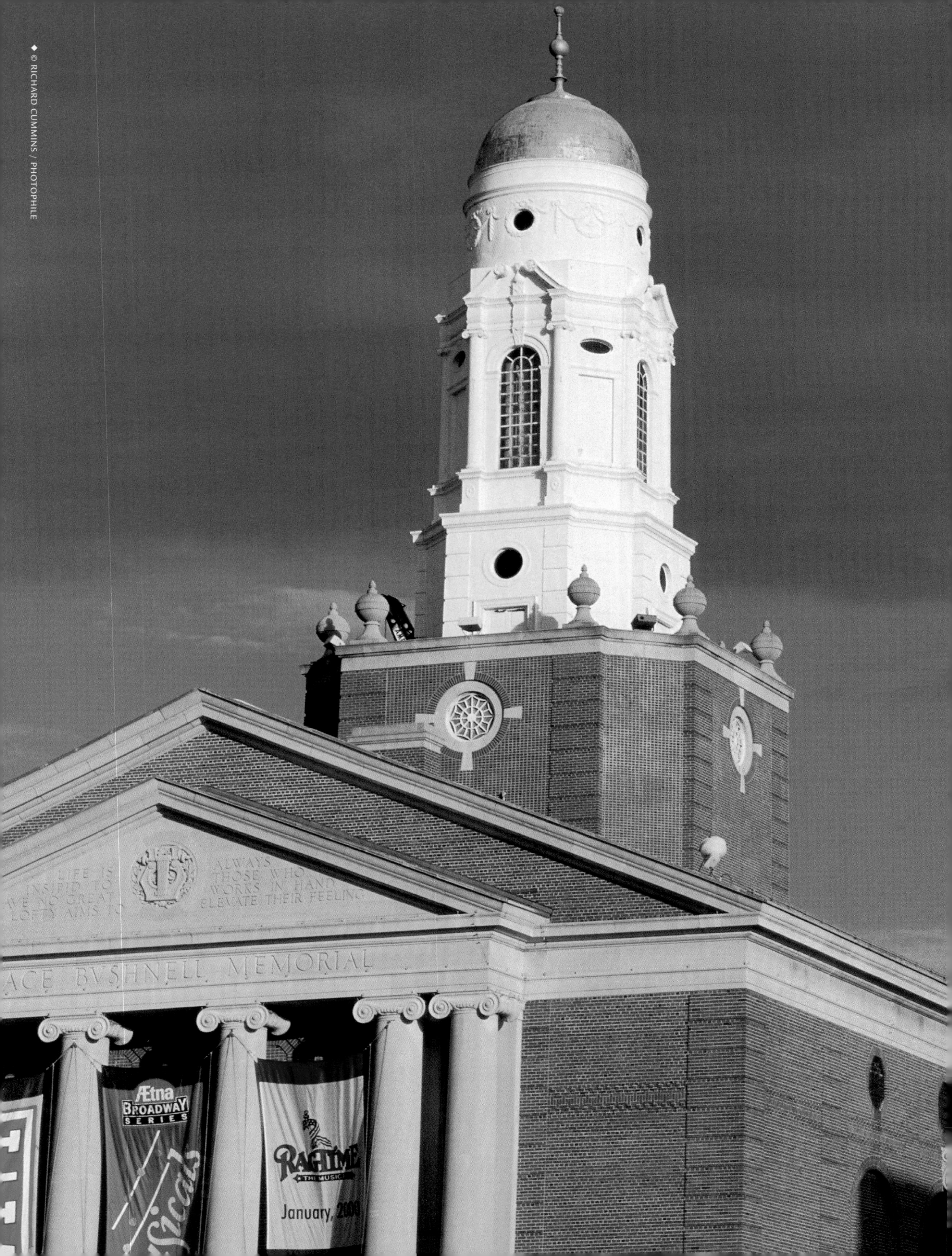

LIFE IS
INSIPID TO   ALWAYS
VE NO GREAT   THOSE WHO
LOFTY AIMS TO   WORKS IN HAND
                ELEVATE THEIR FEELING

ACE BVSHNELL MEMORIAL

ÆTNA
BROADWAY
SERIES

RAGTIME
THE MUSIC

January, 2000

AFTER POPULAR VOTE IN 1854, the citizens of Hartford agreed to finance beautiful Bushnell Park, making it the first in the nation to be paid for with public funds. While many changes have occurred over the years, the park's statuary and landscaping still reflect the ingenuity of its creators.

TRIBUTES TO HARTFORD'S early settlers abound in statues throughout the city. Equally historic is Connecticut's Old State House, capped by a dome featuring a golden replica of Blind Justice.

Revolutionary War re-enactments at the Nathan Hale Homestead in nearby Coventry feature costumes and firearms that make the action seem real—lock, stock, and barrel.

THE BLAST OF A CANNON OPENS and closes each day at Hartford's Old State House, which served as the seat of Connecticut's government from 1796 to 1878 and of the city's government from 1878 to 1915. The building is listed on the National Register of Historic Places and has served as a museum and exhibition hall since 1979.

THE SOLDIERS AND SAILORS Memorial Arch in Bushnell Park was erected in 1886 in honor of those from Connecticut who fought in the Civil War. The arch's intricate sandstone friezes stretch over Trinity Street in downtown Hartford.

A FOUR-ACRE PLOT AT HARTford's Main and Gold streets, the appropriately named Ancient Burying Ground, established in 1640, features around 425 of the original 6,000 grave markers—the majority of them made from brownstone, many with winged skull carvings and engaging epitaphs.

Paying tribute to some of the area's more recently departed, members of Boy Scout Troup 105 place flags at the tombstones of veterans in the Northwood Cemetery (PAGES 52 AND 53).

OUNDED IN 1864, THE 270-acre Cedar Hill Cemetery (LEFT) serves as the burial site for some of Hartford's most famous residents, including gun manufacturer Samuel Colt and Thomas Gallaudet, founder of the American School for the Deaf. Another historical Connecticut resident, Revolutionary War patriot Nathan Hale of Coventry (OPPOSITE), is honored by a statue in front of the Wadsworth Atheneum.

HARTFORD

The Asylum Hill Congregational Church

W HETHER ELABORATE OR
simple, the doorways of the
Greater Hartford commu-
nity open onto a world of hospitality.

THE OPEN ARMS OF HARTFORD'S houses of worship have been welcoming locals since the city's founding. Senior Pastor the Reverend Dr. Barbara E. Headley (OPPOSITE) shepherds one of the city's earliest African-American churches—Faith Congregational Church—which traces its roots to the early 1800s.

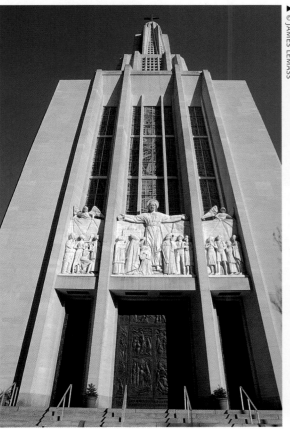

A S THE SITE OF ONE OF THE most famous slavery trials in U.S. history, Hartford was a natural choice for a docking stop during the *Amistad*'s inaugural eastern seaboard tour. Built over a two-and-a-half year period, the reproduction of the Spanish schooner *La Amistad*—the scene of an 1839 slave rebellion at sea—cost around $2.8 million to build.

Some 1 million people visit historic Mystic Seaport each year to see the nation's largest collection of boats and sea-related photography. Located along the Mystic River about 60 miles southeast of Hartford, the community was once a prominent shipbuilding port, believed to have launched some 600 vessels between 1784 and 1919.

HARTFORD'S LOCATION ALONG the Connecticut River lures tourists and boat lovers of all kinds. From April through December, under the watchful eye of its crew—Captain Ed Daniels (OPPOSITE) among them—the *Mark Twain* (BOTTOM) sails from the State Street Landing for daily scenic cruises.

The Mark Twain House (ABOVE) served as the family residence for beloved American author Samuel Langhorne Clemens from 1874 to 1891. Designed by Louis Comfort Tiffany, the 19-room house witnessed the birth of such fictional characters as Tom Sawyer and Huck Finn. The influence of Twain, who borrowed his pseudonym from lingo he had used as a riverboat pilot in his younger days, lives on today as actors like John Pogson (OPPOSITE LEFT) portray him on the stage.

A neighbor to Mark Twain in Hartford's historic Nook Farm area was writer Harriet Beecher Stowe, author of *Uncle Tom's Cabin*. Stowe's personal papers are located in the Stowe-Day Library (TOP), named after the writer and her grandniece, Katharine Seymour Day, who established the Harriet Beecher Stowe Center. The home joins other buildings of architectural significance in the Greater Hartford area.

IN THE IMMORTAL WORDS OF Robert Frost, "Good fences make good neighbors." Those living side by side in Greater Hartford would no doubt agree that neighborliness is a virtue shared by many in the area.

72

OLD FLAGS COME IN A VARIETY of forms—some are faded and tattered, others historic. As one of the original 13 U.S. colonies,

Connecticut—the Constitution State— is represented in a star-studded circle of unity on a replica of the country's very first flag (ABOVE).

W AVES OF IMMIGRANTS arrived in Hartford during the Industrial Revolution of the mid- to late 19th century. The cultural diversity spawned by the changing population remains a prevalent part of the modern city, where an estimated 38 percent of residents are African-American and West Indian American, 39 percent Hispanic and Latino, 22 percent Caucasian, and 1 percent Asian, Native American, or Pacific Islander.

I<small>T MIGHT NOT BE THE REAL</small> thing, but the clans of Connecticut's own Scotland—located about 40 miles east of the city—don the kilts and bagpipes to celebrate the Highland Festival, held each October amid hues of autumn leaves and tartan plaid.

AT GREATER HARTFORD'S annual African-American Parade and Celebration, participants tip their hats to a rich tradition of celebration and wave their banners to progress.

Ɒ VEN UNCLE SAM GETS IN ON THE
clowning around at the annual
Riverfest (TOP), Connecticut's
largest one-day celebration. The event
features four sites—two each in Hartford and East Hartford—along both
sides of the river. For three days every
September, about 250,000 people
attend the Durham Fair to pay tribute
to the state's agricultural roots and to
check out the arts and crafts, livestock,
and midway rides (PAGES 83 AND 84).

ONNECTICUT COMMUNITIES pull their weight when it comes to family fun. In the northeastern corner of the state, the Woodstock Fair (THIS PAGE AND OPPOSITE BOTTOM) occurs each Labor Day weekend, drawing more than 200,000 people to view its agricultural exhibits and ride the midway attractions. In celebration of the grape harvest in late September, the Litchfield Hills Harvest Festival and Craft Show (OPPOSITE TOP), located about 20 miles west of Hartford, gives everybody a chance to participate in some traditional stomping or to sample some of the region's award-winning wines.

No, you aren't exactly seeing double. Of the many achievements made during the 20th century, the controversial act of cloning ranks high on the list. In June 1999, under the guidance of Jerry Yang, scientists at the Transgenic Animal Facility of the University of Connecticut successfully created Amy the cow using cells from her mother's ear. Cloning projects at the former men's agricultural school procure thousands of dollars in research monies.

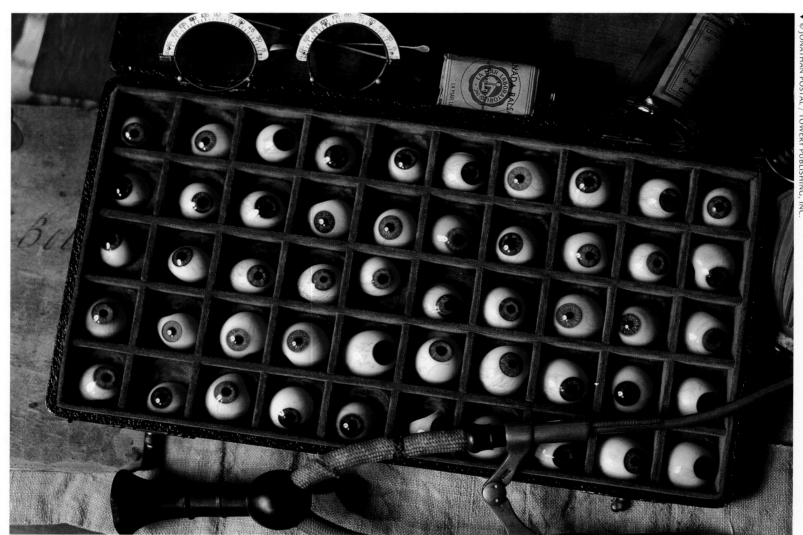

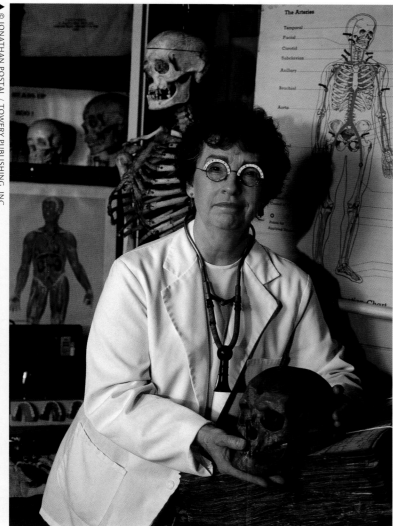

AS EXECUTIVE SECRETARY OF the Hartford Medical Society, Diane Neumann Hernsdorf (LEFT) keeps her eye on the Menczer Museum of Medicine and Dentistry's historic artifacts, where a case of 1870 German-made glass eyes (OPPOSITE) shares shelf space with hundreds of other pieces. At the circa 1797 Joseph Steward's Hartford Museum (RIGHT), located in the Old State House, a 70-million-year-old triceratops horn and a pickled two-headed pig represent just two items in the facility's curiosity collection.

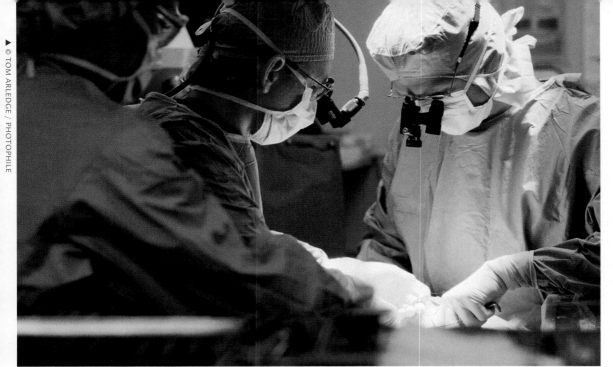

R ESEARCH AND HEALTH CARE go hand in hand at the University of Connecticut Health Center (BOTTOM). Located some 15 miles outside Hartford, the facility boasts a biomedical research center, a hospital, and classrooms for both the medical and dental schools. The city is also home to Connecticut Children's Medical Center, where physicians— including Dr. James Wiley (OPPOSITE), medical director of the emergency department—provide top-notch care to the area's youth. A neighbor to the hospital, historic Trinity College (PAGES 92 AND 93) has been part of Hartford's educational community since 1823.

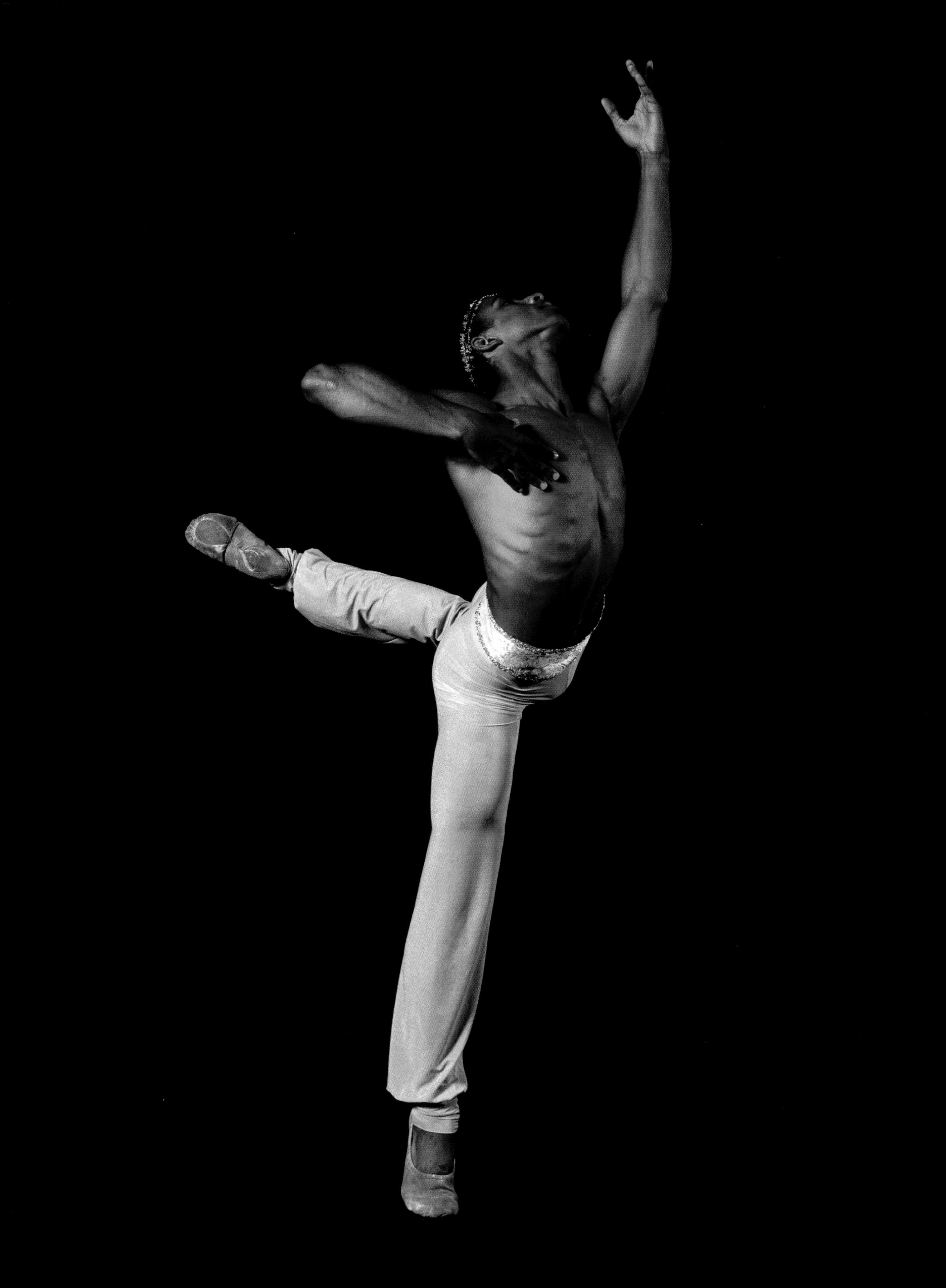

Dance Connecticut, featuring performers such as Dartanian Reed (OPPOSITE) and Emily Crampton (RIGHT), formed in 1999 as the successor to the defunct Hartford Ballet. In addition to its own presentations, the troupe sponsors touring shows and community dance programs.

T HE STRING'S THE THING AT the New England Fiddle Contest at Hartford's Bushnell Park. Begun in 1974, the festival draws more than 5,000 spectators each year to listen to old standards like "The Orange Blossom Special."

IN 1970, JACKIE AND DOLLIE
McLean founded Artists Collective,
an organization that trains Hartford's
inner-city youths in the performing and
visual arts. A gifted saxophonist and
protégé of bebop king Charlie Parker,
Jackie McLean has also become a teacher
and social activist. His wife Dollie—
an actress and dancer—serves as the
collective's executive director.

F OR MORE THAN 40 YEARS, Brad Davis (ABOVE) has put the talk in New England's talk radio market. Each weekday and Sunday morning, listeners can tune in to the *Brad Davis Morning Show* for discussions on everything from politics to music. DJ Kev G (OPPOSITE), a spinner of tunes for both public parties and private events, knows a bit about music himself.

In the Greater Hartford area, the question after work or late at night often becomes: What to drink? Zuzu's Coffee Bar (ABOVE) offers fruit smoothies as well as steaming java cocktails. But if your tastes tend more toward cold and frothy, check out Trout Brook Brewhouse (OPPOSITE), where brewer Jeff Brown also functions as a quality control engineer.

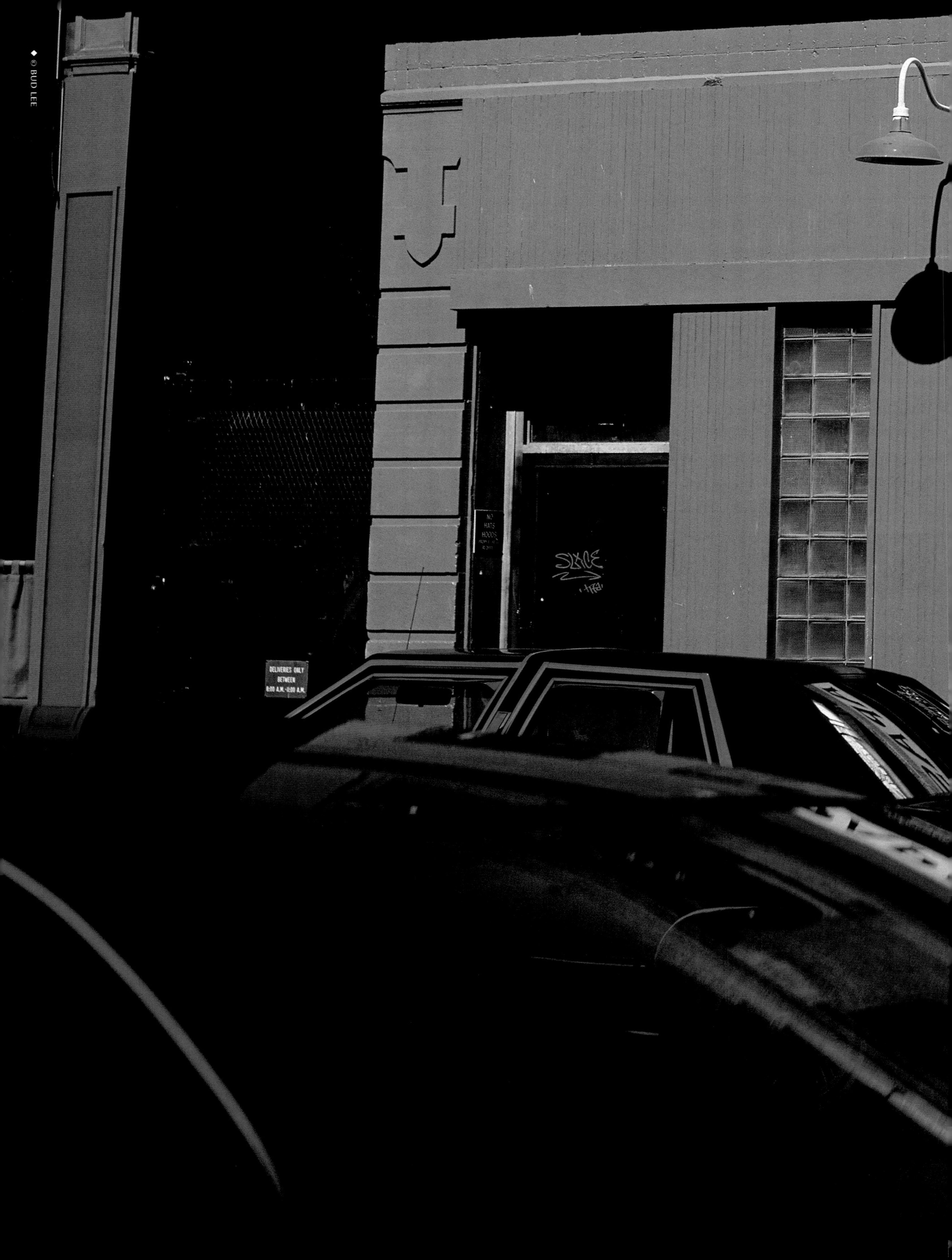

© BUD LEE

PAPAS

PIZZA
RESTAURANT

PIZZA
DINNERS
BREAKFAST

HOT OVEN
GRINDERS

PIZZA

$

USA
TODAY

PIZZA

$

Hartford has a wide array of places to eat, and many won't empty the pocketbook while they pad the waistline. Hal's Aquarius Restaurant & Lounge (ABOVE), Papas Pizza Restaurant (PAGES 110 AND 111), and the city's quiet cafés (PAGES 114 AND 115) cater to the tastes of their diners for breakfast, lunch, and dinner. Even Johnnie Walker (ABOVE, ON LEFT), the owner and operator of Hal's, starts his day the right way, with eggs, coffee—and a refill, of course.

H ARTFORD CLOTHING DESIGNER Anthony Griffin (ABOVE) hopes to inspire the youthful wearers of his fashions to think about the consequences of their actions through his increasingly popular clothing line Heaven or Hell. Ed Johnetta Miller (OPPOSITE) shares messages, too, in the fabrics she weaves, quilts, and paints into works of art. Miller, who has work in the Smithsonian, is also executive director of Opus, Arts & the Aging, a nonprofit group that promotes art experiences for the elderly.

I F THE SHOE FITS, YOU MUST be a member of Hartford's small-business community. Although large corporations may bring in the big bucks for the region, smaller shops featuring everyday services are the soul of the city.

THE CHEESECLOTH-COVERED fields of Windsor hold a surprise: A hand-rolled premium cigar from Connecticut tops the list for many humidor aficionados. Around 3,000 acres of the state are planted in broadleaf and shade tobacco, a hand-picked leaf used for the outer wrapper of cigars. Despite a decline since the 1920s and 1930s, tobacco remains a moneymaker for the state.

BAKED GOODS HAVE ALWAYS earned Hartford businesses a healthy following. George Scott (BOTTOM), the president of Scott's Jamaican Bakery (TOP), offers delicious Jamaican beef patties, coco bread, and other tasty treats to customers who literally line up at the door every day. The focus of Hartford's food industry has always been on quality, even with early establishments like the Honiss Oyster House (OPPOSITE TOP) and other Front Street businesses (OPPOSITE BOTTOM).

J OYOUS OCCASIONS DESERVE the best, and weddings are a chance for families to join together and celebrate. Family-run companies such as Mozzicato-DePasquale's Bakery &

Pastry Shop (OPPOSITE) specialize in cakes and other foods that keep wedding celebrants content. Paolo Mozzicato, Rino Mozzicato, and Carmelo Spino (OPPOSITE, FROM LEFT)

follow in the footsteps of a long line of successful bakers who have kept the company running since 1908.

KNOWLEDGE   HISTORY   JUSTICE

STATE LIBRARY   MEMORIAL HALL   SUPREME COURT

With the words "Knowledge, History, Justice" engraved above its entrance, the State Library and Supreme Court Building (ABOVE) has been witness to a change in the city's approach to sentencing. Under the direction of Community Court Judge Raymond R. Norko (OPPOSITE), in 1998 Hartford implemented an alternative to jail time for minor offenses. Defendants must rake, sweep, and clean up in areas where they committed their crimes. Once the services have been rendered, the charges are dismissed.

Pᴜʙʟɪᴄ sᴀꜰᴇᴛʏ ᴏꜰꜰɪᴄᴇʀs ᴀʀᴇ all smiles during the slow times, but the going gets serious when a crisis strikes. Charles A. Teale Sr. (ᴀʙᴏᴠᴇ ᴄᴇɴᴛᴇʀ), chief of the Hartford Fire Department, heads a dedicated crew of firefighters intent on keeping the city safe. When she's out on the streets, Officer Holly J. Donahue (ᴏᴘᴘᴏsɪᴛᴇ ʀɪɢʜᴛ), a member of the Hartford Police Department, turns to her K-9 companion for support.

Former firefighter Mike
Peters (LEFT) hung up his helmet
after 22 years to take on a new
opportunity in 1993: fighting for his
community as Hartford's mayor.
Built in 1915, the Municipal Building
(OPPOSITE) serves as the seat of city
government.

HARTFORD BOASTS SOME magnificent architecture, particularly in its public facilities. Both the Municipal Building (ABOVE)—with its brick-and-granite exterior and mahogany woodwork—and the Connecticut State Capitol—a High Victorian Gothic structure built in 1878—are listed on the National Register of Historic Places.

O NE SHINING EXAMPLE OF Hartford's success is One Financial Plaza—the Gold Building—glittering on neighboring structures downtown. The 26-story office tower houses banquet rooms and is topped by a heliport.

W HAT MAKES HARTFORD unique? Among its more unusual attributes, the city lays claim to being the birthplace of the first bottled cocktails; the first place where an insurance premium was col- lected; the site of the first typewritten manuscript submitted to a publisher— by Mark Twain, of course; and the home of the first successful jump using a nylon parachute.

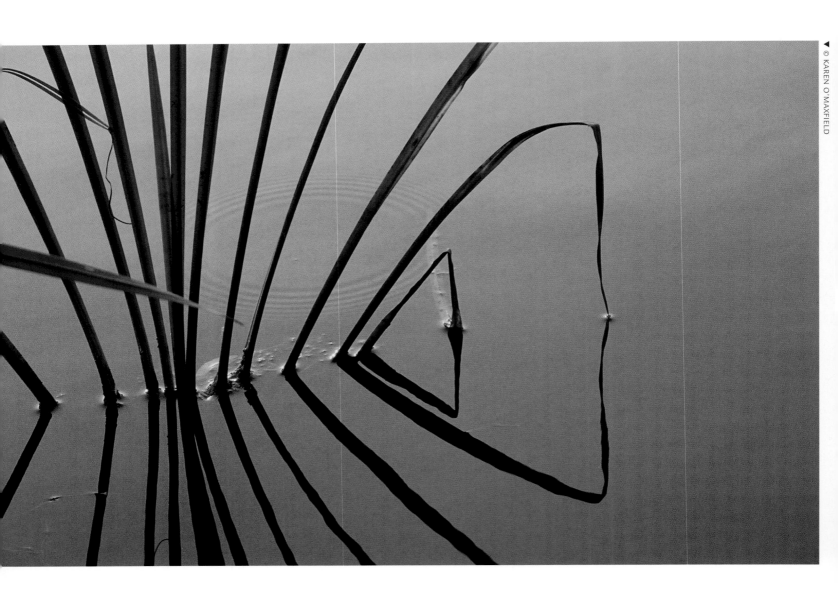

PART OF HARTFORD'S ALLURE lies in its natural beauty. Six major parks in the city help locals get a fair share of the great outdoors.

WHILE PREPARING A CONstruction site in Rocky Hill just south of Hartford, workers came across large three-pronged dinosaur prints. Before they were done, more than 2,000 of the nearly 200-million-year-old footprints were discovered, and state officials established Dinosaur State Park in 1968. Inspired by this historic discovery, local sculptor Alexander Calder created his abstract piece *Stegosaurus* (OPPOSITE) in 1973. The 40-ton commissioned work stands 50 feet tall between the Wadsworth Atheneum and Hartford City Hall.

FROM SYMBOLS OF STRENGTH to faces of fun, big cats are the choice for fair-goers and building entrances alike.

ARTFORD HAS LONG BEEN A baseball town, with fans these days rooting for the Double-A New Britain Rock Cats. An affiliate of the Minnesota Twins organization, the team plays in the 6,146-seat, state-of-the-art New Britain Stadium.

GREATER HARTFORD boxing enthusiasts flock downtown to the newly renovated Dressler Arena/San Juan Center for bouts featuring nationally ranked boxers as well as local favorites including trainer Johnny Duke (PAGE 148) and fighter Greg Cuyler (PAGE 149).

PROFESSIONAL HOCKEY HAS BEEN part of Hartford's sports scene since 1975, when the Hartford Whalers—still memorialized in mural (OPPOSITE)—arrived. Although the Whalers departed, the American Hockey League Wolfpack came to town in 1997 to keep the tradition alive. When not getting their thrills watching others compete in winter sports, locals can take to the slopes for a little skiing or snowboarding.

Dᴜʀɪɴɢ ᴀ HᴀʀᴛFᴏʀᴅ ᴡɪɴᴛᴇʀ, expect freezing temperatures and snow. Workers at Bradley International Airport (ᴏᴘᴘᴏꜱɪᴛᴇ) take deicing measures to make sure passengers depart safely from their facility. With 19 airlines headed to almost 80 cities around the country, Bradley services nearly 6 million passengers a year.

HARTFORD

W HETHER MAN OR BEAST, everybody loves a day when they can be lazy and just soak up the sun or take a leisurely stroll in scenic Greater Hartford (PAGES 154-157).

ARTFORD RESIDENTS SEEKING a fun-filled day trip need travel no farther than Hammonasset Beach State Park in Madison, on Long Island Sound. As Connecticut's largest public beach, the rural park features fields and marshlands—and plenty of good swimming.

I T'S NO FISH TALE: BOATERS ON the Connecticut River often land a big one. But on days when the fish only nibble, at least the view of the city makes for an interesting backdrop.

T HE HISTORY OF TRANSPORTATION takes center stage at the New England Air Museum. Located just 12 miles north of Hartford, the museum rubs shoulders with Bradley International Airport and is the largest indoor aviation museum in the Northeast. The not-always-pleasant past of the railways is preserved in images from the Connecticut Historical Society (PAGES 166 AND 167).

Throughout the year, Lime Rock Park becomes the site for fast and furious auto racing. Located about 50 miles west of Hartford, the track treats spectators to all things automobile, from vintage cars to NASCAR racers.

HARTFORD

GREATER HARTFORD'S VINTAGE car fans are seeing red—classic red, that is. Each year, the Bristol Auto Club draws a crowd for its show at the Mum Festival (TOP LEFT AND OPPOSITE), which features classic coupes and trucks.

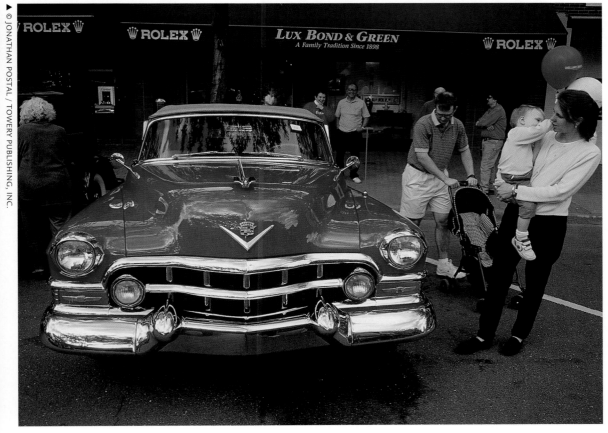

K NOWN AS THE "CAPITAL" OF Western Connecticut, the town of Waterbury is famous for its many historic buildings. Home to some 110,000 residents, Waterbury is also the city where the first Mickey Mouse watch was made—by the Waterbury Clock Company, known today as Timex.

{Profiles in Excellence}

A LOOK AT THE CORPORATIONS, BUSINESSES, PROFESSIONAL GROUPS, AND COMMUNITY SERVICE ORGANIZATIONS THAT HAVE MADE THIS BOOK POSSIBLE. THEIR STORIES—OFFERING AN INFORMAL CHRONICLE OF THE LOCAL BUSINESS COMMUNITY—ARE ARRANGED ACCORDING TO THE DATE THEY WERE ESTABLISHED IN THE HARTFORD AREA.

AETNA INC. ❋ THE ALLIED GROUP INC. ❋ AMERICAN AIRLINES, INC. ❋ ARCHDIOCESE OF HARTFORD ❋ AVON OLD FARMS HOTEL/CLASSIC HOTELS OF CONNECTICUT ❋ BRADLEY INTERNATIONAL AIRPORT ❋ CARRIER CORPORATION ❋ CB RICHARD ELLIS - N.E. PARTNERS, LP ❋ CONNECTICUT CHILDREN'S MEDICAL CENTER ❋ CONNECTICUT MAGAZINE ❋ CONNECTICUT NATURAL GAS CORPORATION ❋ CONNECTICUT STATE UNIVERSITY SYSTEM ❋ CROWNE PLAZA HARTFORD DOWNTOWN ❋ DAY, BERRY & HOWARD LLP ❋ ESPN, INC. ❋ EXECUTIVE GREETINGS, INC. ❋ FAMILYMEDS, INC. ❋ FARMSTEAD TELEPHONE GROUP, INC. ❋ GUIDA'S MILK & ICE CREAM COMPANY ❋ HARTFORD ADVOCATE ❋ HARTFORD BUSINESS JOURNAL ❋ HARTFORD CIVIC CENTER VETERANS MEMORIAL COLISEUM AND EXHIBITION CENTER ❋ HARTFORD OFFICE SUPPLY ❋ HARTFORD PUBLIC LIBRARY ❋ HITCHCOCK CHAIR CO., LTD. & HITCHCOCK FINE HOME FURNISHINGS, INC. ❋ HOSPITAL FOR SPECIAL CARE ❋ JDS UNIPHASE ELECTRO-OPTIC PRODUCTS DIVISION ❋ JETER, COOK & JEPSON ARCHITECTS, INC. ❋ JOSEPH MERRITT & COMPANY, INC. ❋ KONOVER ❋ LOCTITE CORPORATION ❋ THE MAGEE MARKETING GROUP, INC. ❋ MARTINO & BINZER ❋ METROHARTFORD CHAMBER OF COMMERCE ❋ MOORE MEDICAL CORPORATION ❋ OEM OF CONNECTICUT, INC. ❋ OPEN SOLUTIONS INC. ❋ PERMATEX, INC. ❋ PHOENIX MUTUAL LIFE INSURANCE COMPANY ❋ RENSSELAER AT HARTFORD ❋ ROME McGUIGAN SABANOSH, P.C. ❋ SAINT FRANCIS HOSPITAL AND MEDICAL CENTER ❋ SAINT JOSEPH COLLEGE ❋ SHIPMAN & GOODWIN LLP ❋ SIMIONE SCILLIA LARROW & DOWLING LLC ❋ SMITH WHILEY & COMPANY ❋ TAI SOO KIM PARTNERS, ARCHITECTS ❋ TALLÁN, INC. ❋ TRAVELERS INSURANCE ❋ TRINITY COLLEGE ❋ UNIVERSITY OF CONNECTICUT HEALTH CENTER ❋ UNIVERSITY OF HARTFORD ❋ UPDIKE, KELLY & SPELLACY, P.C. ❋ THE WATSON GROUP ❋ WINDSOR MARKETING GROUP ❋ THE WIREMOLD COMPANY ❋ WTIC NEWSTALK 1080 ❋ WVIT-NBC 30 ❋

{1774–1924}

1774   HARTFORD PUBLIC LIBRARY

1799   METROHARTFORD CHAMBER OF COMMERCE

1823   TRINITY COLLEGE

1824   HITCHCOCK CHAIR CO., LTD. &

         HITCHCOCK FINE HOME FURNISHINGS, INC.

1843   ARCHDIOCESE OF HARTFORD

1848   CONNECTICUT NATURAL GAS CORPORATION

1851   PHOENIX MUTUAL LIFE INSURANCE COMPANY

1853   AETNA INC.

1864   TRAVELERS INSURANCE

1886   GUIDA'S MILK & ICE CREAM COMPANY

1897   SAINT FRANCIS HOSPITAL AND MEDICAL CENTER

1908   JOSEPH MERRITT & COMPANY, INC.

1919   DAY, BERRY & HOWARD LLP

1919   SHIPMAN & GOODWIN LLP

1919   THE WIREMOLD COMPANY

Hartford Public Library

{ **S**HEDDING ITS IMAGE AS A MERE BOOK-STORAGE FACILITY, THE PUBLIC library of the 21st century is an exciting civic, cultural, and educational institution that greatly influences a community's quality of life. The mission of the Hartford Public Library, which consists of a central library, nine neighborhood branches, and Library on Wheels, explains the modern library's unique role: "To promote and }

support literacy and learning, to provide free and open access to information and ideas, and to help people participate in our democratic society."

Hartford's library houses extensive cultural, educational, and support programs, as well as the Hartford Collection of the city's rich history, a patent and trademark library, and a comprehensive public resource of fine arts information and popular culture.

The library is funded by the City of Hartford, state and federal grants, corporate and foundation grants, donations, and endowments. With more than 610,000 visitors a year, it is Greater Hartford's top tourist attraction by attendance, according to the *Hartford Business Journal*.

Family Outreach

To help improve reading readiness and achievement, the library begins with family literacy programs, such as one in which three- and four-year-olds receive library cards and learn about libraries. Members of the staff also lend literacy kits to parents, visit day care centers and home day care providers, and teach parents about library resources.

In neighborhood Homework

Centers, students can complete school assignments and teenagers can learn to use technology and gain research skills. Adults interested in consumer health topics can access nearly 10,000 periodicals, reports, and databases. The library also helps adults pursue occupational goals and helps immigrants achieve goals for citizenship and literacy.

Responding to community needs, the central library and four of its branches are open until 10 p.m. Staff at the central branch are available by telephone, computer, and fax until midnight.

Always Evolving, Always Learning

Built in 1957, the Hartford Public Library is experiencing an exciting rebirth in the form of $40 million in capital improvements. The library will be renovated for 21st-century electrical and mechanical systems, air-conditioning for personal comfort, and climate controls to preserve its collections.

A 44,000-square-foot expansion of the central library began to take shape in October 1999. A three-story wing is being built, with a children's floor overlooking the Connecticut River. Library amenities

will include a state-of-the-art community meeting room, 50 computer workstations, a multimedia area, and a learning lab. At the Cyber Café, customers will be able to meet friends, use PCs, and buy books.

When complete, the new library will house Hartford Community Access Television, adding another dimension to the Hartford Public Library's multitude of resources. A 90-car parking lot will accommodate an influx of visitors. On Main Street, a three-story Window of Light will symbolically open the library to the community as a gateway to learning for all.

In 1999, *Library Journal* gave the Hartford Public Library a Library of the Year Special Mention for service to the community, creativity, and innovation and leadership. That same year, the Connecticut Library Association honored Louise Blalock, chief librarian since 1994, with its Outstanding Librarian award.

Blalock has infused the library with a contagious energy, and is credited for its enhanced services and renewal. She envisions an extraordinary future for Hartford's library and fervently believes that "it must never stop evolving, never stop learning, never stop building community relationships."

HARTFORD PUBLIC LIBRARY HOUSES A LARGE MULTIMEDIA COLLECTION (TOP).

IN THE LIBRARY'S NEIGHBORHOOD HOMEWORK CENTERS, STUDENTS CAN COMPLETE ASSIGNMENTS AND LEARN TO USE TECHNOLOGY (BOTTOM LEFT AND RIGHT).

GARY LEWIS

GARY LEWIS

FOUNDED IN 1823, TRINITY COLLEGE IN HARTFORD IS AN INDEPENDENT, nonsectarian, coeducational liberal arts college that enrolls approximately 2,000 undergraduates. Its rigorous curriculum is firmly grounded in the traditional liberal arts disciplines and marked by an array of interdisciplinary studies, exceptional offerings in science and engineering, and distinctive educational connections with Connecticut's capital city

and cities around the world. An extensive community outreach program and an internship program provide Trinity students uncommonly rich opportunities to extend classroom learning, explore potential careers, and make a difference on campus and in the community.

A diverse selection of innovative academic programs is a hallmark of the college, where students can pursue 35 majors, eight of which are interdisciplinary. Among its many other distinctions, Trinity is one of only two top-ranked liberal arts colleges in the nation whose bachelor of science in engineering program has full professional certification.

Highly selective and recognized as one of the top liberal arts colleges in the nation, Trinity attracts students of the highest caliber. Believing that diversity makes learning flourish, the college enrolls students from many different ethnic and cultural backgrounds, enriching the campus community with a diversity of outlooks and experiences.

The heart of a Trinity education is the close personal encounters and intellectual partnership between professor and student. While the first calling of Trinity professors is the instruction of undergraduates, they are also esteemed scholars. For example, Professor Joan Hedrick received a Pulitzer Prize for her biography of Harriet Beecher Stowe, and the Institute for Scientific Information recently ranked Trinity as one of the top liberal arts colleges in the nation for scholarly publications by faculty in biomedical sciences, engineering, and natural sciences.

The college offers numerous study-away opportunities, including Trinity campuses in Rome and in San Francisco, as well as links with universities and foreign study programs on five continents. Trinity is also developing a network of global learning sites in such places as Cape Town; Kathmandu; and St. Augustine, Trinidad.

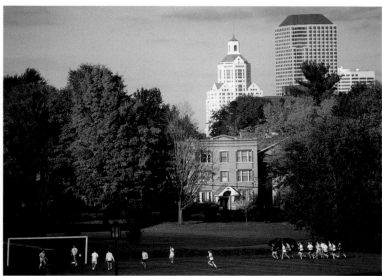

THE HARTFORD SKYLINE LOOMS IN THE BACKGROUND AS TRINITY COLLEGE STUDENTS PARTICIPATE IN NCAA DIVISION III ATHLETICS.

Trinity students enjoy many extracurricular offerings. More than half of the student body participates in intercollegiate athletics and about as many join in an active intramural program. Students interested in the arts find Trinity a congenial home for studying and participating in drama, music, film, musical theater, dance, and the studio arts.

Trinity embraces its Hartford location as an educational resource. The college has established links with the city's museums, theaters, and musical venues. Each year, more than one-third of the student body joins with faculty in ongoing community service projects. And Trinity maintains 200 internships in regional businesses, social service and government agencies, law offices, hospitals, and museums, providing unparalleled opportunities to test classroom learning in the real world and to explore future careers.

In recent years, Trinity has acquired a national reputation for honoring a profound sense of obligation to Hartford. "The college does not wish to be an island within the city, nor an ivory tower with walls so high they are impossible for our neighbors to scale. We intend to draw our neighbors in, not drive them away," Trinity

President Evan S. Dobelle asserts. Collaborating with residents, city and state leaders, and its partners in the Southside Institutions Neighborhood Alliance (SINA), Trinity is spearheading an ambitious neighborhood revitalization initiative designed to create a safe, viable, and vibrant neighborhood that is also a central hub of educational, health, family-support, and economic-development activities.

AT TRINITY COLLEGE, STUDENTS DEVELOP CRITICAL THINKING AND ANALYTICAL SKILLS IN COURSES SUCH AS NEUROSCIENCE. ASSOCIATE PROFESSOR OF PSYCHOLOGY SARA A. RASKIN SHOWS STUDENTS THE EQUIPMENT USED IN RESEARCH ON THE BRAIN.

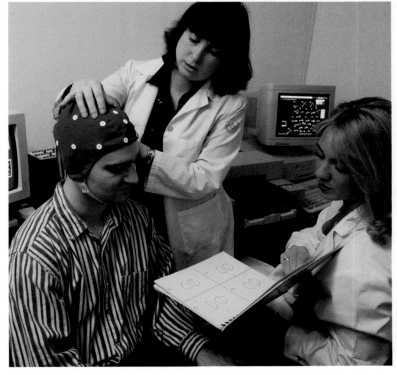

MetroHartford Chamber of Commerce

IN 1799—SOON AFTER HARTFORD BECAME THE SEAT OF STATE GOVERNMENT and built Connecticut's first State House—the city's business leaders formed a mercantile association to resolve disputes and promote business and charitable activities. Today, what is now called the MetroHartford Chamber of Commerce is beginning its third century of advancing the region's economic, civic, and cultural way of life for those who live, work, or visit the capital region.

The Dutch fur traders and Puritans who settled the region on the fertile banks of the Connecticut River could not have imagined that it would become a capital of insurance and aviation companies and, today, home to a growing software and high-technology economy. As the area has evolved, so too has the MetroHartford Chamber of Commerce.

Extending Its Reach

From promoting business and charity, the chamber went on to successfully court large out-of-state companies to relocate to Hartford. Today, believing that a city is only as strong as its region and that the region cannot survive without its center city, the chamber has expanded its boundaries.

With some 4,000 members, the MetroHartford Chamber of Commerce now includes chambers in Avon, Bloomfield, Canton, Farm-

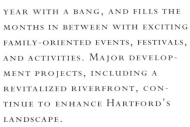

HARTFORD BEGINS AND ENDS EACH YEAR WITH A BANG, AND FILLS THE MONTHS IN BETWEEN WITH EXCITING FAMILY-ORIENTED EVENTS, FESTIVALS, AND ACTIVITIES. MAJOR DEVELOPMENT PROJECTS, INCLUDING A REVITALIZED RIVERFRONT, CONTINUE TO ENHANCE HARTFORD'S LANDSCAPE.

ington, Newington, Rocky Hill, Simsbury, and Wethersfield. Each suburban chamber has its own local programs, but teams up with the MetroHartford Chamber on issues of regional importance. As the hub of the network, the MetroHartford Chamber provides management services to participating chambers, and helps them network and share ideas. About 80 percent of the MetroHartford Chamber's members are small to midsize businesses, with more than half belonging as a result of membership in a suburban chamber.

A belief in regional cooperation led the chamber to be a founding force in the formation of the Capital Region Growth Council, Leadership Greater Hartford, and the Capital Region Partnership, all of which work to improve the area's economic vitality.

As its physical boundaries have grown, the chamber also has assumed a broader leadership role. Perhaps no other organization has been more involved in setting the region's long-term direction and resolving critical issues related to improving the area's business environment and quality of life.

Making Good Ideas Work

Whenever matters of importance to the region's economy are at stake, the MetroHartford Chamber of Commerce is not afraid to take a

leadership role, even on controversial issues. When Connecticut was in a deep recession in the 1990s, the chamber fought for a state income tax and spending cap. The ultimate passage of both measures eliminated a sizable budget deficit, reduced the state's sales tax, and reversed an economic slide.

The chamber addresses the broad issues that form an economic infrastructure, such as transportation, workforce development, education, health care, and tax and fiscal policy. It works to maintain a strong presence at the Connecticut State Capitol and Hartford City Hall. The chamber is a most powerful voice for the local and regional business community.

In addition, the chamber is working with regional organizations and the state's Department of Transportation on a regional transit strategy, including development of a mass transit busway system along the Hartford-New Britain railroad corridor to relieve congestion, and creation of a shuttle system for downtown Hartford. The chamber successfully lobbied for a new passenger terminal at Bradley International Airport, and is working for approval of direct international flight service.

To ensure the quality of life and a strong business climate in Hartford, the MetroHartford Chamber of Commerce strives to improve the

public schools. The chamber-led Citizens Committee for Effective Government is working on issues raised after the state took over the school district in 1997. In another education initiative, the chamber is addressing tight labor markets, technological advances, and other challenges by working as part of a national team to advance legislation that will enhance computer resources in the region's schools. The chamber is also working to restore adequate funding and Medicare reimbursement levels to the region's teaching hospitals.

In the state legislature, the chamber is urging a renewed commitment to controlled spending and competitive taxation policies. The chamber actively supports development efforts in downtown Hartford—such as the Higher Education Center, Riverfront Recapture's pedestrian access facilities, and the convention center—and endorses charter revision for the City of Hartford.

Growing Strong through Volunteers

Like any organization, the Metro-Hartford Chamber of Commerce is as strong as its members are. Only with the continued financial and personal commitments of active members can the chamber continue to protect the interests of businesses in southern New England's economic, cultural, and social center.

The chamber encourages members to contribute their talent, time, and enthusiasm to dozens of important initiatives by planning and working at events, serving on task forces and committees, and lending their professional expertise to priority projects.

Volunteers support economic development through business out-

reach efforts, recognize outstanding business leaders, encourage development of technology-based businesses and activities, analyze state transportation initiatives, and help build leadership skills that give women opportunities to make significant contributions to the region. Important events such as the chamber's annual meeting, Business Expo, the chamber's Golf Classic, the Economic Summit & Outlook conference, and networking activities would not succeed without the hard work of member volunteers.

With the ongoing commitment of its member companies, volunteers, and staff, the MetroHartford Chamber of Commerce will continue to evolve and accept new responsibilities to continue its 200-year tradition of working for a better way of life in the MetroHartford region.

CORPORATIONS AND BUSINESSES HAVE BEEN STRONG SUPPORTERS OF THE MISSION, PROGRAMS, AND ACTIVITIES OF THE METROHARTFORD CHAMBER OF COMMERCE SINCE 1799.

The Hitchcock Chair Co., Ltd. & Hitchcock Fine Home Furnishings, Inc.

SINCE 1824, WHEN LAMBERT HITCHCOCK BEGAN MAKING FANCY chairs in a northwestern Connecticut village, Hitchcock furniture has been a symbol of American ingenuity and fine craftsmanship. The Connecticut native transformed humble maple, birch, and oak through the use of fine finishes, elaborate stencil designs, and complementary striping. Yet America's most famous chair maker is remembered as much for revolutionizing furniture making as for his artistry.

Manufacturing Traditions: Innovation and Quality

In the early 19th century, furniture was made one piece at a time. Observing that Connecticut's clock makers machine-tooled large quantities of standardized parts, Hitchcock had the idea of mass-producing interchangeable chair parts. In that way, beautiful furniture could be crafted in quantity without sacrificing handcrafted quality and at affordable prices. He closed his small woodworking shop and built a mill, and soon his workers were turning out as many as 15,000 chairs a year—using common turned legs and rungs, while varying stenciling, seat backs, seat materials, and finishes.

Today, The Hitchcock Chair Co., Ltd. maintains its heritage of consistent quality, but has added modern efficiencies, including techniques used by other industries. With state-of-the-art manufacturing and a new, just-in-time production approach, the company has significantly reduced delivery time from 16 to four weeks, achieving the timely delivery that customers of high-quality furniture desire.

Hitchcock also employs modern productivity techniques such as cross-training, so more workers know how to do more tasks on a variety of machines. The company has found that increasing employees' knowledge of their craft and reducing monotony greatly improve job satisfaction. Hitchcock is proud of its skilled employees, many of whom have been with the company for more than 20 years.

As Hitchcock dramatically improves production time, it never compromises quality and craftsmanship. The company still uses Lambert Hitchcock's original furniture designs and stencils, and even goes so far as to purchase quill brushes from a company in Austria because they enable artists to apply long stretches of fine striping in a single motion. Hitchcock's craftspeople continue to be innovative, creating new styles and products—such as the latest European collection, Maison Rustique—to meet the needs of modern consumers.

Ten Full-Line Furniture Stores

Hitchcock is one of the few successful companies in the furniture business that is vertically integrated. By owning its manufacturing and retail operations, the firm is able to control its business—from product development through delivery to the customer.

Hitchcock Fine Home Furnishings, showrooms in Connecticut and Greater Boston are the retail operation for the company's timeless wooden chairs, tables, hutches, clock cases, cabinets, and other furniture.

While continuing to sell the handsome stenciled chair that Lambert Hitchcock designed 176 years ago, the showrooms offer several styles of Hitchcock furniture, each a tribute to the company's legacy of fine workmanship. The lines include Hitchcock Classic maple furniture; the Signature Series of

collectible, limited-edition chairs; a formal Berkshire Cherry group; the Shaker-inspired Pleasant Hill collection; American Homestead; and Maison Rustique, furniture with a European country accent.

Besides offering the Hitchcock brand, Hitchcock Fine Home Furnishings carries a full line of fine furnishings. Colorful, upholstered sofas; stuffed ottomans; soft leather sofas; complete dining room ensembles; full bedrooms; and even children's furniture are attractively grouped with complementary hand-knitted rugs, lamps, mirrors, and other decorative accessories. These furnishings come from carefully selected manufacturers, each of whom meets Hitchcock's exacting standards. Mattresses and box springs, for example, are manufactured with eight-way hand-tied strings, literally some of the finest construction in the world.

In-Home Design Service

Amid impressive displays of finely crafted furniture, interior sales consultants offer welcome assistance by taking time to identify each customer's needs. The team of in-home interior design consultants at Hitchcock Fine Home Furnishings—trained to help customers achieve their dream of a beautiful home—offers additional services. By visiting customers' homes and understanding their goals and lifestyles, the skilled design consultants can help them select appropriate furniture, and will recommend rugs,

lamps, and accessories that will make a dream a reality.

In Connecticut, Hitchcock Fine Home Furnishings stores are found in Glastonbury, Orange, Riverton, and Wilton. In 2000, Hitchcock went outside its home state and more than doubled its retail operation, opening six showrooms in Greater Boston, a strong, strategic market. In celebration of recent openings in Burlington, Danvers, Natick, Norwood, and Pembroke, Massachusetts; and in Nashua, New Hampshire, every Hitchcock Fine Home Furnishings showroom was renovated and redesigned to accommodate new lines of furnishings.

Due to its retail expansion, innovative and timeless designs, and devotion to quality and customers, Hitchcock is growing. Only the finishing area remains in Riverton— once known as Hitchcocks–ville— while the corporate offices and manufacturing and assembly operations are in nearby New Hartford. Estimates are that the current workforce of 250 employees will grow to 400 in five years.

As the company moves into the 21st century, its furnishings continue to be cherished, for to own a piece of Hitchcock furniture is to own a piece of American history.

CLOCKWISE FROM TOP LEFT: HITCHCOCK FINE HOME FURNISHINGS' SHOWROOMS FEATURE FULLY ACCESSORIZED VIGNETTES.

HITCHCOCK'S IN-HOME DESIGN CONSULTANTS TAKE TIME TO IDENTIFY THE NEEDS OF EACH CUSTOMER.

HITCHCOCK'S HOME PLANNING SERVICE CAN HELP CUSTOMERS CREATE COMPLETE ROOMS THAT INCORPORATE FURNITURE, AREA RUGS, LAMPS, AND DECORATIVE ACCESSORIES.

Archdiocese of Hartford

FROM ITS EARLY ROOTS, AS POOR IMMIGRANTS STRUGGLED TO ESTABLISH a Catholic church in Connecticut more than 150 years ago, the Archdiocese of Hartford has become an influential part of the community that reaches out to individuals and families in need with love and charity. ❋ In 1829, Bishop Fenwick of Boston bought an abandoned church and founded the Church of the Most Holy and Undivided Trinity at the corner of Main

and Talcott streets. He dispatched Father Bernard O'Cavanagh to Hartford, where the young man made his home on the dirt floor of the basement.

A New Church Is Born

As America prospered in the next decades, a wave of Irish immigrants moved into Hartford and other cities to help build canals and support a building boom. In spite of strong anti-immigrant feeling—No Irish Need Apply—the Irish population and church grew. Despite their own poverty, parishioners helped found seven parishes in Connecticut and western Massachusetts. In 1843, Pope Gregory XVI formally established the new Diocese of Hartford, to include Connecticut and Rhode Island. Concerned because less than 2 percent of the Connecticut population was Catholic, Bishop William Barber Tyler made his seat in Providence.

As Holy Trinity blossomed, the parish built a new brownstone church, St. Patrick. In 1853, during another wave of bigotry, a

MOST REVEREND DANIEL A. CRONIN, S.T.D., ARCHBISHOP OF HARTFORD, INITIATED THE OUTREACH PROGRAM IN 1997 (TOP).

THE CATHEDRAL OF ST. JOSEPH IN HARTFORD WAS DESTROYED BY FIRE IN 1956. WITH THE SUPPORT OF THE COMMUNITY IT WAS REBUILT AND CONSECRATED AGAIN IN 1962 (BOTTOM).

mysterious fire destroyed the old church building.

When the Connecticut-Rhode Island diocese split in 1872, Bishop Francis McFarland made Hartford his seat. The Catholic population in the city was shifting westward. The bishop bought property on Farmington Avenue for a new cathedral, residence, and convent for the Sisters of Mercy. Irish women who were employed as domestics by old Hartford families generously supported the construction fund.

In 1892, Bishop Lawrence McMahon consecrated the stunning St. Joseph Cathedral, which was completely destroyed by fire on December 31, 1956. The distraught community rallied under the fundraising campaign Fire Destroys, Faith Rebuilds. Auxiliary Bishop John Hackett consecrated the new, modern cathedral in 1962.

Today, 750,000 Catholics, or 41 percent of the population, are members of the archdiocese. The Most Reverend Daniel A. Cronin, S.T.D., installed as the third archbishop of Hartford on January 28, 1992, re-

mains the Catholics' spiritual leader in the state of Connecticut.

Furthering Christ's Mission

More than 25 Archdiocese of Hartford ministries and agencies serve God's people throughout Hartford, New Haven, and Litchfield counties. Each furthers Christ's mission by addressing the spiritual, educational, and charitable needs of its people.

Catholic Charities/Catholic Family Services, the largest private social agency in the diocese, promotes the capacity for self-help, with special emphasis on the most vulnerable and disadvantaged. Its broad spectrum of licensed and accredited services—offered at more than 40 sites and in 14 languages—includes family crisis intervention, adoption, drug and alcohol abuse treatment, tutorial programs, refugee resettlement, welfare-to-work services, early childhood development centers, and many more. With the support of volunteers and staff members, Catholic Charities serves people regardless of race, religion, ethnic heritage, gender, disability,

sexual preference, or age.

To meet the needs of the present diverse population, in the city of Hartford alone, Mass is celebrated in French, Spanish, Haitian, Creole, Italian, Polish, Portuguese, Lithuanian, and Vietnamese.

Sharing Blessings

Through the Outreach Program instituted by Cronin in 1997, the Church of Hartford also supports community charities. The church has provided funding to more than 150 recipients in 47 towns; the organizations include food banks, homeless shelters, and counseling centers.

One beneficiary of the Outreach Program, Tabor House, provides a wholesome, safe, and loving home for people living with HIV/AIDS who would otherwise be homeless. The focus is on the residents' total well-being—physical, emotional,

social, and spiritual—so they can live out their lives with the highest quality of life possible.

The Archdiocesan Ministries and Outreach charities continue their good works through the generosity of tens of thousands of parishioners who follow Christ's example of sharing their blessings. In 2000, parishioners donated more than $6.3 million through the Archbishop's Annual Appeal.

Founding the K of C, Informing the Faithful

In 1882, a New Haven parish priest, Father Michael J. McGivney, founded the Knights of Columbus (K of C), now the largest benevolent and fraternal society of Catholic men in the world. McGivney, whose cause for sainthood began in 1996, was first assigned to St. Mary's Church in New Haven, where he ministered to the

widows and children of Irish workers and founded the K of C. In 1884, the Waterbury native transferred to St. Thomas Church in Thomaston, where he died of tuberculosis at age 38.

The *Catholic Transcript* is the second-oldest Catholic newspaper in the nation, yet it was not the Hartford area's first Catholic publication. The *Connecticut Catholic* was founded in 1876—even before Holy Trinity Church—and published for most of the next 10 years. In 1896, Bishop Tierney bought it, made it the official newspaper of the diocese, and changed the name to the *Catholic Transcript* in 1898.

The Archdiocese of Hartford looks to the future with the conviction that its tradition of faith, education, and service will continue to inspire and enrich the diverse citizens of its diocese well into the new millennium.

SERVANT OF GOD, FATHER MICHAEL J. McGIVNEY, FOUNDED THE KNIGHTS OF COLUMBUS IN 1882 (LEFT).

ST. FRANCIS HOSPITAL AND MEDICAL CENTER IS LOCATED IN HARTFORD (RIGHT).

FATHER ROBERT D. BERTIN, DIRECTOR OF THE CATHOLIC DEAF APOSTOLATE "SIGNS" SUNDAY MASS FOR THE HEARING IMPAIRED.

Connecticut Natural Gas Corporation

{ F }OR MORE THAN 150 YEARS, CONNECTICUT NATURAL GAS (CNG) has provided its customers with reliable, efficient, clean, and economical natural gas. Through innovative programs and strategic partnerships, CNG is striving to promote this environmentally friendly energy source as an alternative to other fuels. ✹ Back in 1848, when Mark Twain lived on Farmington Avenue in Hartford,

CNG began providing natural gas to illuminate the city's streets and homes. Before long, the fuel began to be used for heating and cooking, as well. Today, natural gas heats and cools major office buildings, powers electric generating plants, and is a clean alternative fuel for automobiles.

Award-Winning Environmentalism

The country's first commercial district heating and cooling (DHC) system is owned and operated by CNG's affiliate, The Energy Network (TEN). This closed-loop system heats and cools 16 million square feet of residential, commercial, and retail space in more than 70 buildings in the Hartford area.

DHC is environmentally friendly in that it uses cogeneration, which captures and makes use of "waste"

AL FERREIRA

HUNTER NEAL

DENNIS TANNERY

energy from making electricity. As a result, DHC lowers fossil fuel use, reducing both the emissions that cause acid rain and the carbon dioxide production that leads to global warming. And because DHC serves a large number of buildings from a single, central plant, DHC reduces the CFC emissions that are destroying the ozone layer. Environmentalists around the world hail the energy efficiencies provided by DHC, and many European nations have created strategies that feature DHC as an integral piece of their long-term energy plan.

Here in the United States, federal, state, and local governments have also begun to support the use of DHC. In fact, the EPA gave one of the buildings on TEN's loop, One State Street, an Energy Star Building Award in 1999. This award—the first in New England—recognized TEN's efforts to prevent pollution by deploying products and technology that use less energy.

A Clean Alternative to Gasoline

In partnership with automobile manufacturers such as Honda and Ford, CNG has taken a lead in encouraging local taxi companies, delivery services, and police depart-

ments to adopt a fuel-efficient, cost-effective, environmentally friendly means of transportation: natural gas vehicles. Today, the police cars in Rocky Hill, Newington, and Berlin are powered by natural gas, as are more than 100 UPS delivery trucks in Greater Hartford, the State Capitol Police Force fleet, and more than half of the taxis in downtown Hartford.

New Conservation Technologies

Through TEN, CNG is constantly investigating new conservation technologies, such as cogeneration, which uses the heat produced during the production of energy as a source of energy for other functions, including heating water. The result is an environmentally friendly, high-efficiency means of conserving energy and budgets. One of TEN's largest cogeneration plants powers Hartford Hospital.

By providing a clean source of energy, constantly developing innovative ways to provide energy, and encouraging local businesses, residents, and municipalities to find ways to conserve, CNG continues to serve the environment and more than 145,000 customers in 22 communities.

IN 1853, A GROUP OF INVESTORS IN HARTFORD'S NEWEST FIRE INSURANCE business looked halfway around the world to name their company. They found inspiration in Mount Etna, an active volcano in Sicily, since a volcano, although surrounded by fire and smoke, is itself not consumed. The firm was incorporated as Aetna Life Insurance Company. ✹ Aetna's name proved prophetic from the start. Of the 19 insurance companies

formed in the United States between 1850 and 1854, only Aetna and two others survived. Since its founding, the firm has endured and prospered due to its remarkable ability to re-invent itself, time and time again.

In the 1990s, Aetna achieved a strategic transformation rare among companies of its size and longevity. The firm sold its individual life business and property-casualty business units; acquired U.S. Healthcare, which *Fortune* magazine dubbed "America's hottest HMO"; and acquired NYLCare Health Plans and Prudential Health-Care. A new company, Aetna Inc., emerged, providing nearly 47 million people worldwide with quality products, services, and information to help them manage their health and financial well-being.

Early in 2000, Aetna was in the process of separating into two distinct companies—one focusing on health care insurance, the other on financial services. This change signaled yet another exciting direction in Aetna's evolution, while retaining the link to its heritage and roots in Hartford.

A Caring Attitude

When Aetna outgrew its downtown Hartford headquarters and built a new home on Farmington Avenue

in 1930, it included a store, bowling alleys, tennis courts, and other amenities for its employees. That caring attitude continues to this day, and employees nationwide have access to health, retirement, life, and other insurance benefits;

fitness programs; diversity networks; and more. *Working Mother*, *Working Woman*, and *Latina Style* magazines, among others, have named Aetna a top employer.

Aetna is renowned for its philanthropy as well. The company generously supports the education and welfare of the community as well as the arts, such as the Bushnell in Hartford; Hartford Symphony; National Gallery of Art in Washington, D.C.; and other fine arts organizations. Aetna supports health-related campaigns, such as those mounted by the American Heart Association and National Colorectal Cancer Alliance; contributes to numerous charitable organizations; and sponsors events that promote diversity, including the National Conversation on Race, Ethnicity and Culture. Every year, Aetna and its employees are among the largest contributors to both the local arts council and United Way.

AETNA INC. PROVIDES NEARLY 47 MILLION PEOPLE WORLDWIDE WITH QUALITY PRODUCTS, SERVICES, AND INFORMATION TO HELP THEM MANAGE THEIR HEALTH AND FINANCIAL WELL-BEING.

AETNA'S HARTFORD HEADQUARTERS IS THE WORLD'S LARGEST EXAMPLE OF GEORGIAN ARCHITECTURE.

A LEADING PROVIDER OF INSURANCE, INVESTMENTS, AND TRUST services, Phoenix Home Life Mutual Insurance Company has been a symbol of financial strength, stability, leadership, and citizenship in Hartford for nearly 150 years. The company has become a leader in wealth management, guided by principles of high standards for ethical business conduct, exceptional customer relations

and services, and respect for people. Today's sophisticated products and services are several generations away from what began as a simple life insurance business.

Phoenix uses its special expertise to help business owners, senior corporate executives, and high-net-worth individuals accumulate, preserve, and transfer their money. Whether clients want to earmark money for a favorite charity, save for retirement, or leave a lasting legacy to heirs, Phoenix will offer solutions and strategies to help them achieve their dreams.

Phoenix, a Fortune 500 company, is one of the nation's largest mutual life insurers and a leading money manager through Phoenix Investment Partners, Ltd. In addition to mutual funds, the firm's products include individually managed accounts, qualified plans, and variable annuities. Phoenix provides complete fiduciary and investment services through Phoenix Charter Oak Trust Company, and offers the assistance of a full-service broker-dealer and registered investment adviser through WS Griffith and Co.

Life Insurance for Teetotalers

Believing that there were enough teetotalers in the area in 1851 to support an insurance business, a group of Hartford's prominent business, religious, cultural, and civic leaders formed the American Temperance Life Insurance Company. Applicants had to pledge total abstinence from alcohol, with the policy voided if the applicant broke the pledge.

Shrewdly, the new company hired well-known temperance lecturers as agents and became quite successful. By the onset of the Civil War 10 years later, the temperance movement was waning and it was clear that there were not enough abstainers to support the business. In 1861, the company welcomed the nontemperate and changed its name to Phoenix Mutual Life Insurance Company.

The company had been formed on a joint stock and mutual basis. After a brief scandal that involved a shareholder gaining controlling interest and selling options on his shares to two men of dubious distinction, the board of directors and the stockholders voted to close the stock transfer books in 1889 and make Phoenix a wholly mutual company.

A History of Innovation

Phoenix was innovative from the start, creating services and products that set the standard. A dedicated sales force was created, widening Phoenix's geographical scope to become a national company. In 1901, the firm published *The Field*, a periodical for agents and one of America's first employee communications efforts. Phoenix also began holding regular regional conferences for agents and annual meetings for general managers. In 1906, a "prospectus and 10 lessons upon life insurance" was bought from one of Phoenix's general agents, and the firm developed the first training course for agents ever used by a life insurance company. Phoenix began pioneering new marketing techniques in 1912, including the first known direct mailing to obtain sales leads. The company's national advertising campaign in 1928 stressed the need for retirement income, and for many years Phoenix was known as the retirement income company. One ad said, "You don't have to be rich to retire at 55 on $200 a month."

Following World War II, the firm's products were increasingly customer-driven. Phoenix began selling group life and health insurance in 1957, pioneering a new concept that allowed small businesses to band together by industry and offer employee benefits that previously were available only to large corporations. Phoenix reentered the life

ROBERT W. FIONDELLA IS CHAIRMAN AND CEO OF PHOENIX HOME LIFE MUTUAL INSURANCE COMPANY (LEFT).

DONA D. YOUNG IS THE COMPANY'S CURRENT PRESIDENT (RIGHT).

insurance brokerage business and developed a competitive distribution system that was so successful that, within 10 years, brokerage accounted for 30 percent of the business and grew to 50 percent by the 1990s.

In the 1950s, Phoenix introduced the family rider policy to provide coverage on the lives of a husband and his wife and children in one contract, and in 1967, the firm became the first national insurer to offer premium discounts to nonsmokers. In 1982, survivorship policies payable on the death of the surviving policyholder were pioneered. From the 1960s through the 1980s, the company got into reinsurance, and began offering investment products and services. The firm also introduced the Phoenix line of mutual funds, which continue to be highly respected. The company's first-to-die policies in the early 1990s recognized the special needs of working couples.

Merger with Home Life

Seeking to grow, Phoenix merged in 1992 with Home Life Insurance Company, another strong contender in the industry, and created Phoenix Home Life. It was a wise match, for the history and success of Home Life closely paralleled that of Phoenix.

Home Life, founded in 1860 in New York City, grew rapidly during the Civil War and capitalized on the postwar westward migration by becoming the first life insurer to remove travel restrictions. In 1893, Home Life built America's first skyscraper, which had 20 floors, opposite New York's City Hall. Later, the company targeted the wealth as a new market and provided discounts through its Preferred Life Plan. That change led to new concepts that continue today—to concentrate on finding financial problems to solve instead of finding prospects to sell—and a belief that relationships could be built between the company and its clients. Home Life entered the growing group insurance market in 1949, when corporations needed excellent benefit packages to attract and retain quality employees.

After the merger, the new company, looking for ways to keep the business strong, introduced Beyond the Numbers, a PC-based tool for agents. This tool described the many forms of life insurance and set the industry standard for easy-to-understand presentations. In 1995, Phoenix

merged its money management subsidiary, Phoenix Securities Group, with Duff & Phelps to create Phoenix Duff & Phelps, and laid the foundation for a new trust business, Phoenix Charter Oak Trust Company. The firm also established Phoenix Realty Group, Inc., a real estate investment management subsidiary.

In 1998, it was clear that direct ownership of real estate and direct mortgage lending no longer made sense for a life insurance company, so Phoenix sold those businesses. The firm began developing a global presence primarily through alliances with companies in Scotland, Argentina, Oman, and Luxembourg.

Phoenix experienced a year of significant achievement and transition in 1999. The company increased its focus on variable products, expanded its variable annuity sales and distribution force, and bought PFG Holdings Inc. of Philadelphia, a private placement variable life and annuity business that serves wealthy individuals. Capitalizing on the

strengths of its core businesses and its solid market position, Phoenix sharpened its strategic focus to provide wealth management strategies for affluent and high-net-worth individuals.

By the end of 1999, Phoenix was stronger than ever. Net gains before dividends and federal income taxes reached a record $533 million, and Phoenix's surplus soared to $1.4 billion—the highest level in its history, up $222 million from 1998. The company's $71.9 billion in assets increased 20 percent over the previous year.

In February 2000, Dona D. Young, who joined the company in 1980, was elected its president, and Robert W. Fiondella continued as chairman and CEO. After carefully reviewing the company's strategic direction, the board of directors authorized management to develop a plan for conversion from a mutual company to a publicly traded stock company in order to strengthen Phoenix's position as a premier

PHOENIX HAS BECOME A LEADER IN WEALTH MANAGEMENT, GUIDED BY PRINCIPLES OF HIGH STANDARDS FOR ETHICAL BUSINESS CONDUCT, EXCEPTIONAL CUSTOMER RELATIONS AND SERVICES, AND RESPECT FOR PEOPLE.

wealth management company. Demutualization, the process of approvals, takes 12 to 18 months to complete.

In Hartford for Good

Phoenix and its 2,000 employees are committed to enhancing the quality of life in Hartford and its surrounding towns. Contributions extend beyond corporate sponsorships and donations to include employees' active participation, and every year more than 100 nonprofit, civic, and educational institutions benefit from their efforts. According to Fiondella, "Profit and good citizenship are compatible for a company devoted to people and the fulfillment of their personal dreams and the dreams of their loved ones."

A major supporter of college basketball, Phoenix is the Official NCAA Insurance and Investment Advisor, and sponsors both the Phoenix Classic, a tournament for NCAA men's teams, and the Phoenix WBCA High School All-America Game for girls. When Connecticut Public Television signed a long-term contract with the University of Connecticut women's basketball team, Phoenix was the first corporation to step to the line as top underwriter.

Phoenix has embraced the Special Olympics, setting an unparalleled standard for volunteerism and commitment. In 1995, close to 60 percent of home office employees and their families volunteered at the Special Olympics World Games in Connecticut to make the event a triumph of goodwill. The next year, the company announced an unprecedented eight-year sponsorship of Special Olympics International. Since then, Phoenix employees in offices across the country have staged fund-raising activities, volunteered at events, escorted players and coaches, kept score, and presented seminars to help families with special needs plan for their financial futures.

Within Hartford, Phoenix is a driving force in making the most of the city's economic, cultural,

PHOENIX OFFICES ARE ALSO HOUSED AT 38 PROSPECT STREET IN HARTFORD.

PHOENIX USES ITS SPECIAL EXPERTISE TO HELP BUSINESS OWNERS, SENIOR CORPORATE EXECUTIVES, AND HIGH-NET-WORTH INDIVIDUALS ACCUMULATE, PRESERVE, AND TRANSFER THEIR MONEY.

educational, and recreational resources. The company is a strong
supporter of Riverfront Recapture,
which is developing the Connecticut
River and its riverfront through a
network of public parks, promenades,
and recreational facilities. Adriaen's
Landing, a major revitalization proposed for the city center—and
conceived by Fiondella—calls for
construction of a convention center,
a hotel, retail stores, an entertainment center, and an attraction—to
be determined—that would be built
on land donated by Phoenix.

As a result of a partnership with
Phoenix, attendance and mastery test
scores have improved at Fred D.
Wish Elementary School in Hartford.
The company loaned an executive
to help develop and implement a
school improvement plan, and funded
teacher training and academic en-
richment. For more than 15 years,
Phoenix employees have tutored Wish
students in math and language skills.

Throughout the city, dozens of
organizations, including the Greater
Hartford Arts Council, Artists Collective, AIDS Ministries of Connecticut, Community Health Services,
Doc Hurley Scholarship Foundation,
Trinity College Boys and Girls Club,
and San Juan Tutorial, are beneficiaries of Phoenix and its community-
minded employees. In 1996, Phoenix
received the Greater Hartford Cham-

ber of Commerce Pride Award
for excellence in community
involvement.

While Phoenix is renowned for
its considerable civic contributions
to the Hartford area, the company
stands out for its blue-green headquarters building as well. Situated
high on a plaza beside the Connecticut
River, the structure is the world's first
two-sided office building. Known locally as the boat building, it is an

apt symbol for a company that helps
customers navigate their financial
futures and is itself preparing to sail
into uncharted waters as a public
company.

In 2001, Phoenix will proudly
celebrate its 150th anniversary with
a simple theme that sums up its contributions to policyholders and their
beneficiaries, producers, employees,
and, of course, the community:
Here for Good, Since 1851.

PHOENIX EMPLOYEES CELEBRATE
THE UNIVERSITY OF CONNECTICUT'S
RECENT NCAA NATIONAL
CHAMPIONSHIP.

A MAJOR SUPPORTER OF COLLEGE
BASKETBALL, PHOENIX IS THE OFFICIAL
NCAA INSURANCE AND INVESTMENT
ADVISOR, AND SPONSORS BOTH THE
PHOENIX CLASSIC, A TOURNAMENT
FOR NCAA MEN'S TEAMS, AND THE
PHOENIX WBCA HIGH SCHOOL
ALL-AMERICA GAME FOR GIRLS.

Travelers Insurance

{ **T**HE RED UMBRELLA OF TRAVELERS INSURANCE—ONE OF AMERICA'S MOST widely recognized corporate symbols—signifies protection, security, and confidence. For more than 135 years, the Hartford-based company has proved to its customers that they're better off under the umbrella. ✺ Today, Travelers is one of the nation's most trusted providers of high-quality insurance and financial products and services, solving

the insurance, asset-accumulation, and income-protection needs of individuals and businesses around the country through a diversified line of products. From property casualty products to life and annuity products and financial services, Travelers has a long-standing tradition of innovation and service.

Extending Its Reach

In 1998, Travelers Group merged with Citicorp to form Citigroup Inc., the world's most global financial services company, serving 100 million customers in 100 countries with insurance, consumer banking, securities brokerage, asset management, and many other products and services. Citigroup's brands include Travelers Insurance, Citibank, Salomon Smith Barney (SSB), SSB Citi Asset Management, CitiFinancial, and Primerica.

Citigroup and Travelers are focused on the future. As part of a strategy to grow in emerging markets, Citigroup has developed alliances to expand into key Asian

▲ JEFFREY YARDIS/CORPORATE IMAGES

markets. As these markets' financial systems develop and the needs of consumers and businesses grow, Citigroup and Travelers will be well positioned to share in that future growth.

Industry Firsts

Travelers, too, has a history of looking forward and of finding innovative solutions for a changing world. In 1864, Travelers became the first company in North America to provide insurance against accidents. In 1897, the company issued the first automobile insurance policy. In 1919, it issued the first air travel insurance. In 1969, Travelers issued the first accident insurance for spaceflight and our nation's landing on the moon. In 1999, the firm offered another first: coverage for expenses related to identity fraud, a fast-growing, technology-age crime. Today, Travelers provides personal insurance for automobiles, homes, boats, and more through 5.4 million policies.

On the commercial side, in 1904, Travelers organized the first corps of safety engineers to help customers control losses, and, in 1965, the firm provided the first commercial package policies for most types of businesses. Today, the company serves nearly a million businesses—from small,

family-run stores to Fortune 100 companies—for their property, casualty, surety, and specialty needs.

In the financial services arena, in 1913, Travelers pioneered the concept of group life insurance. In 1958, the company was the first to offer life insurance at lower rates for women. In 1997, the firm introduced an innovative universal life policy with premiums and features that are competitive with 30-year term products. Today, Travelers is among the country's fastest-growing life and annuity businesses.

And on the service front, in 1968, Travelers established the first employee-staffed claim hot lines to serve its life and annuity customers—a commitment to unsurpassed service that continues today. Following devastating hurricanes, floods, or ice storms, Travelers quickly dispatches teams of claim handlers and catastrophe-response vehicles to the scene to help restore policyholders' lives and property to normal.

Technology As a Competitive Edge

Travelers installed its first computer in 1958 and is now an industry leader in its use of technology. The company's processing and service systems have garnered numerous awards from

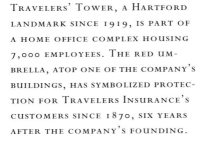

TRAVELERS' TOWER, A HARTFORD LANDMARK SINCE 1919, IS PART OF A HOME OFFICE COMPLEX HOUSING 7,000 EMPLOYEES. THE RED UMBRELLA, ATOP ONE OF THE COMPANY'S BUILDINGS, HAS SYMBOLIZED PROTECTION FOR TRAVELERS INSURANCE'S CUSTOMERS SINCE 1870, SIX YEARS AFTER THE COMPANY'S FOUNDING.

A DYNAMIC WORKFORCE AND SAVVY MANAGEMENT STEER TRAVELERS INTO A THIRD CENTURY AS A CORPORATE LEADER AND INNOVATOR.

◄ JEFFREY YARDIS/CORPORATE IMAGES

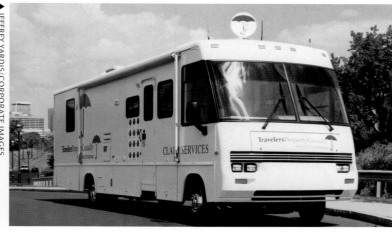

the information technology industry.

Travelers has seized opportunities in the growing world of e-commerce. The nation's top Internet banks, bill management services, and on-line payment services reassure their customers with Travelers' first-in-the-industry coverage for protection against loss from unauthorized on-line transactions.

Citigroup provides customers with an on-line, one-site resource for personal financial data, as well as a one-stop shop for the services of many of the company's businesses, including Travelers. Citigroup is also a preferred provider on many of the most popular Web sites, offering a full range of financial products and services, including Travelers Insurance products.

Caring for the Community

While extending its horizons, Travelers combines philanthropy with business practices that benefit America's communities. The firm's Fair Access program increases availability of insurance for urban residents, and provides minority agents in urban markets with training and other assistance. Travelers is the largest provider of home owners insurance for Habitat for Humanity homes, providing special considerations to new owners in this program.

Travelers and its employees also support their communities with generous donations of money, time, and talent. In 2000, Travelers and Citigroup announced nearly $90 million in long-term financial commitments to Greater Hartford, as well as tens of millions of dollars in Citigroup community development loans. In addition, Travelers makes commitments of many millions of dollars each year to its headquarters city.

Dedicated Travelers employee volunteers contribute to dozens of charities. For 20 years, the company has sponsored a tutoring program for Hartford grammar school students. Volunteer efforts occur wherever Travelers does business throughout the country. In 1999, the National Multiple Sclerosis Society named Travelers Corporation of the Year.

A Company Is Its Employees

Travelers attracts and retains top-notch people by rewarding top performance and offering challenging opportunities, along with the latest technology, training, educational reimbursement, and competitive compensation and benefits, including stock ownership opportunities in the company. With myriad employee benefit programs, Citigroup and Travelers are ranked among the country's most family-friendly companies.

From its origins in accident insurance to its expansion into e-commerce and the international marketplace, Travelers remains an industry leader committed to offering customers the highest-quality protection and services, providing agents and brokers an outstanding company to do business with, and giving employees a gratifying and rewarding place to work.

CLOCKWISE FROM TOP: TRAVELERS AND CITIGROUP ARE RANKED AMONG THE NATION'S MOST FAMILY-FRIENDLY COMPANIES, WITH SERVICES FOR EMPLOYEES THAT HELP THEM BALANCE PERSONAL AND BUSINESS PRIORITIES.

TRAVELERS' IMMEDIATE-RESPONSE CATASTROPHE VEHICLES TRAVEL TO HURRICANES, ICE STORMS, FLOODS, AND OTHER NATURAL DISASTERS TO BRING CARING, ON-THE-SPOT CLAIM SERVICE TO CUSTOMERS.

THROUGH CITIGROUP FOUNDATION, INDIVIDUAL CONTRIBUTIONS, AND EMPLOYEE VOLUNTEERISM, TRAVELERS SUPPORTS COMMUNITY DEVELOPMENT, THE ARTS, AND EDUCATION, SUCH AS AN EMPLOYEE TUTORING PROGRAM THAT HELPS 150 HARTFORD STUDENTS EVERY WEEK.

TRAVELERS BRINGS TOP-QUALITY SERVICE TO CUSTOMERS, AGENTS, AND BROKERS THROUGH A MASSIVE TECHNOLOGY INFRASTRUCTURE.

Guida's Milk & Ice Cream Company

GUIDA'S MILK & ICE CREAM COMPANY—ONE OF ONLY THREE FAMILY-owned dairies remaining in New England—has built a successful business, quart by quart, with its strong work ethic, quality, and honest family values. The company maintains its independence in a rapidly consolidating industry, and business has never been better. ✦ "When my father started in the 1930s, there were 67 dairy farms

in New Britain alone," recalls Alexander Guida III, president and CEO. "Now, conglomerates are buying and consolidating milk processors all over the country. We have decided not to sell—to grow and to remain independent."

Guida's father, Alexander Guida Jr., was one of 13 children of Polish immigrant parents. He began selling milk in New Britain in 1932, at the height of the Great Depression. In 1947, he and his brother Frank bought the milk plant and business from Seibert Dairy, which had been started in 1886. The combined company was named Guida-Seibert Dairy.

Family Name, Company Name

Today, the family business is growing at an unprecedented rate. In 1999, Guida's Milk & Ice Cream had 200 employees. In 2000, it had more than 300. "People are realizing that the conglomerates are not accountable to local customers or farmers, and that our products and services really are better," says Guida. "People prefer to deal with a

local, family business. When they call us, they know a Guida will be there because it's not just our company name, it's our family name. Our customers are part of the family."

In addition to Alexander Guida, company management includes

Bernie Guida, chairman of the board; Michael Guida, executive vice president; James Guida, vice president and secretary; and Michael P. Young, chief financial officer. Many top professionals with experience in the dairy industry are

GUIDA'S COMMITMENT TO QUALITY AND TO CENTRAL CONNECTICUT IS AS SOLID AS ITS INDEPENDENCE.

THE MANAGEMENT TEAM OF GUIDA'S MILK & ICE CREAM COMPANY COMPRISES (FROM LEFT) BERNIE GUIDA, CHAIRMAN; ALEXANDER GUIDA III, PRESIDENT AND CEO; MICHAEL GUIDA, EXECUTIVE VICE PRESIDENT; AND JAMES GUIDA, VICE PRESIDENT. ALSO FEATURED FRONT AND CENTER IS THE GUIDA MASCOT, SUPERCOW. MICHAEL P. YOUNG, CFO, IS NOT SHOWN.

Dairy Field MAGAZINE NAMED
GUIDA'S MILK & ICE CREAM
ONE OF THE TOP 100 DAIRIES
IN THE UNITED STATES IN 1999.

part of the company team as well.

Guida's Milk & Ice Cream Company is one of the largest independent dairy companies in New England. Each month, a fleet of tanker trucks delivers approximately 30 million pounds of milk from dairy farms all over New England and New York to New Britain, home of Guida's processing plant and company headquarters.

Sitting between New York City, Boston, Albany, and Providence, Guida's is the most centrally located dairy plant in New England. Deliveries to New England and New York originate in New Britain, while depots in New London, South Windsor, and Trumbull serve as staging points for deliveries to more distant areas.

Focus on Quality

Guida's quality is hard to top. On average, milk has a shelf life of 12 days, but Guida's is one of the few processors in New England to earn a regulatory approved shelf life of 18 days. The secret is to buy only the best milk locally, to constantly test quality at the farm and plant, and to give close attention to the best manufacturing processes and procedures.

Guida's has a long history as a milk processor, but it also manufactures ice-cream mixes and sells hard ice cream. In addition to the Guida's label, the company distributes major brands such as Häagen-Dazs, Ben & Jerry's, Good Humor, and M&M

Mars. The company also processes a complete line of fruit drinks, orange juice, and spring water.

Up and down the eastern seaboard, Guida's refrigerated trucks deliver milk and ice cream, fruit drinks, and water to supermarkets, convenience stores, schools, hospitals, nursing homes, mom-and-pop stores, restaurants, distributors, airlines, specialty stores, and federal facilities, including the Groton submarine base. A diverse customer base protects Guida from fluctuations in any one market.

Industry Innovator, Community Leader

Guida's Milk & Ice Cream, which *Dairy Field* magazine named one of the top 100 dairies in the United States in 1999, is an industry leader. The company was among the first to use homogenized milk, the first to dispense vitamin-fortified milk from amber bottles, and one of the first to use plastic pints. Guida's also was the first to deliver Tropicana in glass bottles, and is the only milk company that places a tamperproof foil inner seal on its products.

Guida's innovations extend beyond its products to public service. It was the first dairy in the United States to place images of missing children on milk carton side panels, a practice that has spread nationally. Since then, the company has used its milk cartons to salute the University of Connecticut's championship basketball teams and to advertise

job openings. Guida's appealing mascot, known as SuperCow, has been spreading antidrug messages, as well as a variety of public service messages about good nutrition and healthy living since 1995, in her flashy red cape and mask.

Guida's commitment to quality and to central Connecticut is as solid as its independence. With the Guida family's long-standing reputation and its personal stake in the business, the company attracts a high caliber of local employees and treats them like family. The firm is well known for its support of schools, community groups, and charities.

With business growing exponentially, Guida's Milk & Ice Cream is undertaking the largest single expansion in its history. The company has purchased adjacent property and is expanding its cooler warehouse and processing plant. A new maintenance facility and a trailer staging yard have already been completed. These additions will greatly increase Guida's capacity to handle additional products more efficiently. The firm also recently added to its fleet of trucks and initiated a major recruitment drive.

Guida's Milk & Ice Cream Company has pledged to grow and remain independent, and the Guida family is confident that the firm will remain competitive and continue to offer quality products and excellent service. "We're 114 years old, and we're still fresh," Guida says.

Saint Francis Hospital and Medical Center

QUALITY CARE HAS BEEN A HALLMARK OF SAINT FRANCIS HOSPITAL and Medical Center, the largest Catholic hospital in New England, since its founding in 1897 by the Sisters of Saint Joseph. Its excellent balance of quality care and cost efficiency earned it a Top 100 Hospitals in the United States rating in 1997 and 1998 by HCIA, Inc. and William Mercer, Inc., a leading health care consulting firm.

While hospitals traditionally treat a patient's physical ailments, Saint Francis has a broad view of medicine that acknowledges the roles of the mind and spirit in healing. The role of art in healing, for example, is evident throughout the hospital, from its more than 200 original murals, paintings, tapestries, and sculptures, to lectures that inspire creativity, to therapists who use art to help patients express themselves and relax.

A Leader in Diversified Care

Connecticut's third-largest hospital with 617 beds, Saint Francis is widely respected for its women's health, cardiac care, and oncology services.

The hospital has long been a leader in cardiology, having established Connecticut's first coronary care unit in 1965. More recently, in 1991, it opened the Hoffman Heart Institute of Connecticut, the first comprehensive heart institute in southern New England. In addition, Saint Francis was the first hospital in the state to offer port-access surgery, an alternative to traditional open-heart surgery, using tiny incisions and miniature cameras. In 1999, Saint Francis was named a Top 100 Hospital for coronary artery bypass surgery by HCIA, Inc. and William Mercer, Inc.

The hospital has been a pioneer in other areas as well. Saint Francis' cancer program established the region's first outpatient chemotherapy program, in 1981, and the hospital is an active participant in national and international clinical research trials. At the Comprehensive Breast Health Center, the first of its kind in the area, women can get a same-day diagnosis for most suspected cases of breast cancer.

Saint Francis' affiliation with Mount Sinai Hospital in 1990, was the first collaboration between a Catholic hospital and a Jewish hospital in U.S. history. After a formal merger in 1995, Saint Francis established The Rehabilitation Hospital of Connecticut on the Mount Sinai campus. Providing services previously unavailable in the Hartford area—including treatment for traumatic brain injury, stroke, and spinal cord injury—the 60-bed facility complements Saint Francis' designation as a Level I emergency/trauma center.

Community Care

The caring staff at Saint Francis go beyond the hospital's walls with services to improve the health of the community. They work with teenagers on violence prevention, and operate a regional lead poisoning treatment center and a regional child abuse center.

Equally important, the staff provide services to help consumers take charge of their health, including an array of educational programs and complimentary medicine services, a Web site (www.stfranciscare.org), a consumer health information library, and a motor coach called HealthCheck that brings medical services into the community. Saint Francis also is moving services closer to where people live, with Saint Francis Care offices in Avon, Glastonbury, Enfield, and Rocky Hill.

Whether caring for patients at the hospital or reaching into the community, Saint Francis Hospital and Medical Center focuses on the mind, body, and spirit of each individual, as well as the overall well-being of all those it serves.

THE VIEW FROM WOODLAND STREET OF THE BEAUTIFUL MAIN ENTRANCE TO SAINT FRANCIS HOSPITAL AND MEDICAL CENTER, REFERRED TO AS THE PATIENT CARE TOWER

RADIATION ONCOLOGIST RICHARD SHUMWAY, MD, TYPIFIES THE SAINT FRANCIS Care REGIONAL CANCER CENTER'S APPROACH, COMBINING A CARING STAFF WITH THE LATEST IN TECHNOLOGY.

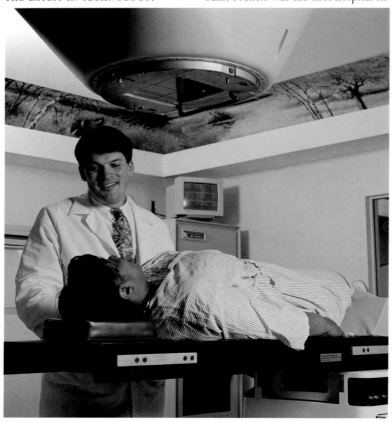

◄ DAN AITCHISON

I N 1900, NOT LONG AFTER THOMAS EDISON BEGAN PAVING THE WAY FOR modern electrical inventions and Alexander Graham Bell invented the telephone, D. Hayes Murphy bought the Richmond Electric Conduit Company and launched what would ultimately become the brand of choice for wire and cable management and power and data quality systems. ✸ Sixteen years later, Murphy sold the first product under the Wiremold®

brand name: the 500 series metal raceway. The raceway, a thin metal channel, secured and protected electrical wiring and delivered easy, on-wall access to power. The product found a receptive market, and in 1926, the business became known as The Wiremold Company.

Wiring a building for telephones, faxes, cable TV, video, and computer networks is a challenge, complicated by rapid changes in technology. Increasingly, traditional, behind-the-wall wiring will not work because it is not flexible. To this evolving market, The Wiremold Company introduced the concept of wire and cable management. Wiremold systems are now modular, accessible, and expandable, and allow building owners to avoid costly reconfiguration of their wiring systems.

Offering Innovative Solutions

Throughout the years, new product development has been a proven growth strategy for The Wiremold Company. The firm introduced the first dual channel raceway for power and low-voltage phone wire. It created an overhead lighting system, which for the first time allowed industrial and retail users to support and energize overhead

lighting with a single strut system. And the company spearheaded development of a new architectural raceway that now combines both form and function. Today, Wiremold solutions help future-proof buildings because few are designed to accommodate all current and future cable technologies.

Since the late 1980s, acquisitions have fueled company growth in the United States and abroad. Wiremold bought the leading U.S. in-floor wire management company, Walker Systems Inc., as well as several specialty companies in the United Kingdom and Eastern Europe. These strategic acquisitions have allowed the company to broaden its family of wiring solutions well beyond the traditional on-wall category.

The Wiremold Company now offers commercial, industrial, and residential customers the widest range of wire and cable management solutions in the industry. It is the only company that offers complete solutions, including perimeter raceways, in-floor systems, and overhead cable tray.

A Model of Manufacturing Excellence

The Wiremold Company is respected for more than its leading product lines. Under the leadership of Art Byrne, president and CEO, the company has adopted the Kaizen philosophy of continuous improvement. In fact, the firm is considered a model of manufacturing excellence, attracting top American and foreign manufacturers to its West Hartford headquarters to observe the Wiremold Production System in action.

Beginning its second century, The Wiremold Company continues to respond to customers' ever changing needs. Therefore, the company is strategically positioned to offer "the only way to wire" for schools, businesses, and homes.

THE WIREMOLD COMPANY NOW OFFERS COMMERCIAL, INDUSTRIAL, AND RESIDENTIAL CUSTOMERS THE WIDEST RANGE OF WIRE AND CABLE MANAGEMENT SOLUTIONS IN THE INDUSTRY.

Joseph Merritt & Company, Inc.

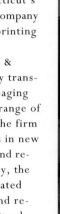 OSEPH MERRITT & COMPANY, INC.—ONE OF THE LEADING GRAPHIC imaging companies in southern New England—can print almost anything on almost any kind of material, whether it is a floor mat, an overhead banner, a wall mural, or even a delivery truck. By remaining open to change in the marketplace and staying abreast of cutting-edge technologies, the company has flourished for more than 90 years. ❋

Joseph Merritt & Company started simply in 1908, providing Hartford-area manufacturers with engineering services from the design stage to blueprinting. As Connecticut's towns and cities grew, the company remained primarily a blueprinting service bureau.

In 1987, Joseph Merritt & Company began to radically transform itself into a digital imaging enterprise with a growing range of services. Thinking ahead, the firm invested millions of dollars in new technology and equipment and retrained its employees. Today, the company's customers—located throughout the New England region—include the architectural, engineering, construction, manufacturing, graphic design, and legal communities.

First on Many Fronts

Joseph Merritt & Company boasts a number of firsts that are commensurate with the firm's reputation in the graphic imaging business. The company was the first in the area to offer LightJet digital photo printing. The Cymbolic Sciences LightJet 5000 offers the ultimate in color fidelity for large-format graphic imaging. Joseph Merritt & Company also bought the first Canon laser color copier in New England and helped to develop the color copy

market. The firm's state-of-the-art copiers can produce nearly 5,000 full-color copies per hour. The company was also the first beta test site in New England for a new Canon Bubble Jet copier that led to the subsequent development of a large-format color copy market.

The largest blueprint company between New York and Boston, Joseph Merritt & Company was the first in the Northeast to offer customers clean, environmentally

sound, plain-paper copies "blueprints" in lieu of traditional ammonia-based copies. The firm has nine high-volume, automatic plain-paper copiers with collating capabilities. These copiers are digitally fed from network servers to produce engineering drawings. Joseph Merritt & Company remains the largest supplier of engineering and drafting supplies in the state of Connecticut.

In 1990, the company was the first service bureau to offer DocuTech Electronic Press printing for quick, economical black-and-white printing jobs such as newsletters and manuals. Now, the firm has four digitally fed presses. In 1993, Joseph Merritt & Company became one of only 12 authorized fabricators in the world—and the first in Connecticut—for 3M™ Scotchprint™ Graphics. These adhesive-backed, high-resolution graphics can be applied to nearly any surface, and can withstand ultra-violet rays and extreme weather conditions. Joseph Merritt & Company can provide everything from design help to installation.

The company's range of capabilities includes custom trade show displays,

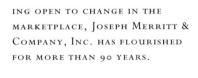 BY STAYING ABREAST OF CUTTING-EDGE TECHNOLOGIES AND REMAINING OPEN TO CHANGE IN THE MARKETPLACE, JOSEPH MERRITT & COMPANY, INC. HAS FLOURISHED FOR MORE THAN 90 YEARS.

WITH SIX STRATEGIC LOCATIONS, JOSEPH MERRITT & COMPANY IS NEVER MORE THAN AN HOUR AWAY FROM ITS CUSTOMERS IN SOUTHERN NEW ENGLAND.

booths, and graphics. Thanks to its commitment to digital imaging and the concept of just-in-time printing, the firm's achievements have not gone unnoticed: Joseph Merritt & Company received the Greater Hartford Technology Business Leader of the Year Award in 1995.

Another Bright Idea

Joseph Merritt & Company's Bright Ideas Gallery at its Hartford headquarters displays all of the company's products, services, and imaging capabilities. Graphics are hung from ceilings and are wrapped around chairs, columns, floors, walls, and even buses and trucks, allowing customers to compare the range of choices available. Also showcased in the impressive, 5,000-square-foot exhibit is the variety of materials these images can be produced on, as well as the different laminates and finishing options. The Bright Ideas Gallery also displays information on Joseph Merritt & Company's history and the evolution of graphic imaging. Business associations and groups can use the gallery and conference room for meetings and gatherings.

With six strategic locations—in Hartford, Danbury, New Haven, New London, Waterbury, and Providence—Joseph Merritt & Company is never more than an hour away from its customers in southern New England. The company's high-speed wide area network (WAN) ensures

that the transfer of images and documents from one location to another is nearly instantaneous.

Nationally recognized, Joseph Merritt & Company continually reestablishes industry standards by introducing new technologies that improve product quality and solve

customers' evolving imaging and reprographic needs. With dedication to quality in every endeavor and a cutting-edge approach, the innovative company will continue to adapt and grow with changing technology and changing client needs for generations to come.

JOSEPH MERRITT & COMPANY'S BRIGHT IDEAS GALLERY AT ITS HART-FORD HEADQUARTERS DISPLAYS ALL OF THE COMPANY'S PRODUCTS, SERVICES, AND IMAGING CAPABILITIES.

TODAY, THE COMPANY'S CUSTOMERS INCLUDE THE ARCHITECTURAL, ENGINEERING, CONSTRUCTION, MANUFACTURING, GRAPHIC DESIGN, AND LEGAL COMMUNITIES.

Day, Berry & Howard LLP

FOUNDED IN 1919 AND DEDICATED TO THE COMMUNITIES IT SERVES, Day, Berry & Howard LLP—the largest law firm in Connecticut and one of the largest in New England—conducts a full-service practice from its Hartford birthplace and its Stamford, Greenwich, and Boston offices. The firm's clients run the gamut from large corporations to closely held businesses and individuals. ❋ Day, Berry & Howard strives to

deliver superior client services. Unlike many large law firms, it rewards its attorneys for collaboration, giving clients the advantages of its experienced staff and diversified practice. However big the team, one responsible partner—available to collaborate with the client at all times—closely monitors and assures client satisfaction with the firm's attorneys and the work they perform.

Some clients have been with the firm for decades, and as their businesses and legal requirements have evolved, Day, Berry & Howard continues to expand its capabilities to meet their needs. Excellent support services—including more than 55

paralegal assistants and modern law libraries managed by professional librarians—facilitate the firm's ability to serve clients. The firm's commitment to providing superior technological support is evidenced by its in-house, computerized litigation and precedent retrieval system, as well as a recent major investment in technology enhancement of research capabilities.

Giving Back to the Community

Attorneys are most often seen in the courtroom or boardroom. But at Day, Berry & Howard, they also can be found installing wallboard, teaching teenagers peer mediation skills, and serving the community in a variety of other ways.

The firm strongly believes in sharing its talents for the public good and encourages each of its more than 230 attorneys to perform at least 50 hours of community work annually—most give much more.

Day, Berry & Howard also has a long history of contributing legal services in matters large and

small. It was the first law firm in New England to fully sponsor a Habitat for Humanity house, and contributed funding and its enthusiastic staff to the inner-city project, which was completed in 1999. In addition, attorneys have worked with high school students on mock trial programs and apprenticeships, and incorporated the Latino Foundation of Stamford, Inc. to support a training and scholarship program in the media and arts.

A Department to Fit Every Client Need

The firm's attorneys provide representation and counseling spanning a full range of matters, from technology and intellectual property, emerging companies and commercial litigation to individual clients, utilities, institutional finance, and government investigations, to name a few.

Day, Berry & Howard's Technology and Intellectual Property Law attorneys represent a diverse group of companies and individuals

ATTORNEYS AT DAY, BERRY & HOWARD LLP PROVIDE REPRESENTATION AND COUNSELING SPANNING A FULL RANGE OF MATTERS, FROM TECHNOLOGY AND INTELLECTUAL PROPERTY, EMERGING COMPANIES AND COMMERCIAL LITIGATION TO INDIVIDUAL CLIENTS, UTILITIES, INSTITUTIONAL FINANCE, AND GOVERNMENT INVESTIGATIONS.

in transactions and litigation. The firm represents a number of the largest and best-known technology companies in the world, as well as new and emerging ventures built on intellectual property and technology.

The Emerging Growth Companies practice represents emerging growth companies and investors in fields such as information technology and telecommunications, biotechnology, health care management, and health care information systems. Day, Berry & Howard is a renowned authority in the field, and clients benefit from its attorneys' wide-ranging contacts, including institutional and private venture capital and debt financing sources.

The Commercial Litigation department is one of the largest trial practices in New England. Day, Berry & Howard has a total of seven partners who are Fellows of the American College of Trial Lawyers, more than any other firm in New England. Commercial litigation work generally involves trials and appeals throughout New England's federal and state courts and administrative hearings throughout the United States. When it serves a client's interests, attorneys recommend and assist in alternative dispute resolution proceedings in lieu of litigation.

The firm's Individual Clients attorneys advise individuals in connection with the transfer of wealth from one generation to the next in a tax-efficient manner. The firm is particularly active in succession planning for business owners, including developing strategies to facilitate transfer of ownership with minimum taxation. A very active Probate

Litigation group coordinates efforts with the Individual Clients practice in representing the interests of fiduciaries and beneficiaries of estates and trusts.

With New England's preeminent utilities practice, attorneys in the Utilities Practice Group are experienced in every aspect of utility-related legal work, and participate in proceedings before state regulatory commissions, the Federal Energy Regulatory Commission, the Nuclear Regulatory Commission, and the Securities and Exchange Commission.

The Institutional Finance department of Day, Berry & Howard works primarily on a national scale and provides legal services to a broad range of financial institutions. The department includes lawyers who

have substantive expertise in structured finance; secured transactions; unsecured lending and private placements; equipment leasing; project, utility, and real estate finance; and institutional equity investment workouts, restructuring, and investment and securities law.

The Government Investigations Practice Group represents clients on criminal, civil, and regulatory investigations conducted by federal and state agencies. The team includes the former U.S. attorney for Connecticut and former federal and state prosecutors, giving clients the benefit of lawyers who have conducted, and now defend against, such investigations.

As Day, Berry & Howard enters a new century, it continues to serve the community and its clients—as it has for more than 80 years—by providing experience, knowledge, and cutting-edge technology while operating under the highest levels of quality and teamwork.

DAY, BERRY & HOWARD WAS ONE OF THE FIRST LAW FIRMS IN NEW ENGLAND TO FULLY SPONSOR A HABITAT FOR HUMANITY HOUSE.

FOUNDED IN 1919 AND DEDICATED TO THE COMMUNITIES IT SERVES, THE FIRM STRIVES TO DELIVER SUPERIOR CLIENT SERVICES.

Shipman & Goodwin LLP

{ **O**NE OF CONNECTICUT'S LARGEST LAW FIRMS, SHIPMAN & GOODWIN LLP has been serving clients for more than 80 years. Although the full-service firm was founded by Hartford's leading citizens in 1919, it continues to bring a progressive and energetic approach to the practice of law. The firm is committed to understanding clients' needs and priorities, and to producing practical and }

effective solutions to legal problems. Long-standing relationships are a matter of great pride, and the firm's attorneys strive to achieve an ongoing role of counselor and business partner.

Shipman & Goodwin is large and diverse enough to handle the most sophisticated work, yet small enough to care for each client individually. The firm's six departments—Business, Litigation, Labor and Employment, Real Estate, Taxation, and Trusts and Estates—form the framework for delivery of legal services by an extremely broad range of practice groups that offer clients interdisciplinary teams with experience and expertise.

Shipman & Goodwin's clients reflect the impressive diversity of its practice groups. The firm's cli-

ents include most of Connecticut's school districts, as well as venture capital firms, banks, environmental services, franchises, governments, health care centers, manufacturers, insurance companies, and nonprofits. One exciting area of growth is the firm's work with Connecticut's emerging high-tech industry. Shipman & Goodwin has helped many new ventures throughout their development, from initial financing to initial public offering, besides assisting more established companies.

Shipman & Goodwin attorneys appear in state and federal courts, and before administrative agencies throughout Connecticut and across the country. In addition to Connecticut-based businesses, the firm regularly represents national corporations for litigation of nationwide

scope, and represents out-of-state corporations in local litigation. Where clients operate extensively in regulatory environments, the firm has developed cross-disciplinary teams of lawyers who understand the particular industry.

Far-Ranging Practice Groups
As general counsel to a wide range of businesses, Shipman & Goodwin advises its clients in such diverse areas as commercial finance, banking law, venture capital, health care law, environmental law, and international law. The firm has extensive experience in the formation of businesses, securities law, corporate governance, corporate finance, and contracting, and is frequently involved in major corporate transactions.

SHIPMAN & GOODWIN LLP'S SIX DEPARTMENTS—BUSINESS, LITIGATION, LABOR AND EMPLOYMENT, REAL ESTATE, TAXATION, AND TRUSTS AND ESTATES—FORM THE FRAMEWORK FOR DELIVERY OF LEGAL SERVICES BY AN EXTREMELY BROAD RANGE OF PRACTICE GROUPS THAT OFFER CLIENTS INTERDISCIPLINARY TEAMS WITH EXPERIENCE AND EXPERTISE.

Shipman & Goodwin has created several industry-based practice groups such as the Health Care Fraud and Abuse Group. This group has developed a national practice representing insurers and others in the health business interested in pursuing fraud, racketeering, or benefit abuse claims.

Shipman & Goodwin also serves as bond counsel to the State of Connecticut and various political subdivisions. As special counsel to the Connecticut Development Authority, the firm has significant experience in financing program legislation and agency procedures and regulations.

The firm has extensive experience in representing management in all aspects of labor relations and employment law. For more than 50 Connecticut cities and towns, Shipman & Goodwin represents governmental employers in municipal and school law matters, labor relations, and employment issues. Attorneys review proposed personnel policies and actions for compliance with state and federal statutes, applicable regulations on equal employment opportunity, and exceptions to employment-at-will rules.

The firm also handles complex real estate transactions and matters of international, federal, state, and local taxes. Shipman & Goodwin assists with a variety of situations where tax consequences are central, from international transfer pricing to small-business succession planning. The firm offers estate, financial, and tax planning services, as well as will contests and related work.

Shipman & Goodwin was the first law firm in Connecticut to develop a Web site, located on the Internet at www.shipmangoodwin.com. The firm has enhanced its Internet presence by offering a convenient means for potential recruits, other attorneys, and clients to communicate with the firm.

A Tradition of Caring

Thanks to the legacy of its early-20th-century founders, Arthur Shipman, Charles Goodwin, and George Day, Shipman & Goodwin has been infused with a tradition of caring that embraces clients, the community, and employees.

In 1994, Shipman & Goodwin donated $100,000 in legal services to the City of Hartford and organized a book drive that delivered more than 2,000 textbooks to Hartford schools. Shipman & Goodwin performs an annual volunteer project where the attorneys spend one full day outside the office working directly at the volunteer site. Employees also serve their communities through board memberships, as advisers to government, and by donating time to organizations.

The Connecticut Bar Association has recognized the firm for promoting diversity through workplace rules. As early as 1940, Lillian Malley was named a female partner in the firm. In recent years, Shipman & Goodwin has undertaken a broadening of talent to ensure that the firm will continue to provide the best service to its growing and diverse roster of clients.

Having tripled in size since 1970, Shipman & Goodwin is one of Connecticut's fastest-growing law firms; it has offices in Stamford and Lakeville, and occupies seven floors in the Phoenix building in Hartford. After more than eight decades, Shipman & Goodwin continues serving its clients with distinction.

SHIPMAN & GOODWIN IS LARGE AND DIVERSE ENOUGH TO HANDLE THE MOST SOPHISTICATED WORK, YET SMALL ENOUGH TO CARE FOR EACH CLIENT INDIVIDUALLY.

{1925-1960}

1925   WTIC NewsTalk 1080

1929   The Watson Group

1932   Saint Joseph College

1936   Jeter, Cook & Jepson Architects, Inc.

1938   Connecticut Magazine

1941   Bradley International Airport

1941   Hospital for Special Care

1947   Moore Medical Corporation

1950   Hartford Office Supply

1952   American Airlines, Inc.

1953   Loctite Corporation

1953   WVIT-NBC 30

1955   Avon Old Farms Hotel/

        Classic Hotels of Connecticut

1955   Rensselaer at Hartford

1957   University of Hartford

1959   Konover

WTIC NewsTalk 1080

WTIC NewsTalk 1080 has been broadcasting since 1925, thanks to a Travelers Insurance Company executive who thought radio could attract business. From the start, WTIC has been an innovator. In 1926, the station made the first public broadcast from an airplane and was the first to originate live broadcasts of vaudevillians. In 1929, it installed a 50,000-watt transmitter, allowing it to attract listeners as far away as Australia.

Personalities of Note

WTIC has a history rich with personalities, most notably Bob Steele. Hired in 1936, he hosted *The Bob Steele Show* for nearly 50 years. With Steele's dry wit and offbeat features, the program was often the nation's number one morning show, with an average of 500,000 listeners. Still active today, Steele hosts the morning show the first Saturday of each month.

Another WTIC icon is Arnold Dean, who joined the station in 1965. Dean has had many roles during his tenure at WTIC, including the broadcast of play-by-play, color commentary, and analysis. He is widely considered Connecticut's top sports broadcaster. Although semiretired, Dean hosts *Sports Talk,* a nightly call-in show, and gives afternoon sports updates twice a week.

Currently, the informative *Ray Dunaway Show* with Diane Smith is Connecticut's number-one-rated morning show. Dunaway has been with WTIC since 1992; Smith, a former local TV reporter, joined him in 2000. The program provides listeners with all the information they need to start their day: news, weather and traffic reports, sports, and discussion of the issues that affect listeners' lives.

In 1993, WTIC capitalized on its reputation as a trusted news source and changed its programming, becoming WTIC NewsTalk 1080. Today, it is the place to turn for local news coverage, special programs, school/business closings, and local talk shows.

WTIC is an affiliate of the Boston Red Sox Radio Network and is the flagship station of the University of Connecticut's UCONN Radio Network. WTIC produces and originates play-by-play broadcasts for close to 100 UCONN football and men's and women's basketball games each year, heard on WTIC and other affiliate stations.

BRYAN CURTIS

At the Forefront of Public Service

WTIC has always been community minded. On July 6, 1944, when 168 people were killed and nearly 700 others were seriously injured in Hartford's Great Circus Fire, WTIC announcers on the scene knew their live impressions would panic listeners. Acting responsibly, they elected to quell rumors, and opened their facilities to the Red Cross and police authorities.

The station's 1944 series on alcoholism was the first of its kind; and in the late 1940s, Allen Ludden's show for young people, *Mind Your Manners,* was picked up nationally, winning a Peabody Award. In 1954, the station's first afternoon telephone talk show, *The Miller Party Line,* initiated a format that has become a mainstay of AM radio.

In 1990, WTIC opened the 1080 Fund to raise money for the Greater Hartford Salvation Army. Through the years, it has evolved into the Holiday Store program, which collects food, clothing, toys, and donations for the Salvation Army and the people of Connecticut each December. WTIC supports countless other local charities, including the Fidelco Guide Dog Foundation, Jimmy Fund, Riverfront Recapture, Connecticut Children's Medical Center, Juvenile Diabetes Foundation, and Susan G. Komen Breast Cancer Foundation, among many others.

Now a proud CBS Radio/Infinity Broadcasting station, WTIC NewsTalk 1080 upholds its tradition of excellence. Today, WTIC, an important voice in southern New England for 75 years, continues to be a beacon of public service and innovative programming.

The informative Ray Dunaway Show with Diane Smith is Connecticut's number one-rated morning show. Dunaway has been with WTIC since 1992; Smith, a former local TV reporter, joined him in 2000.

Today, WTIC NewsTalk 1080 is the place to turn for local news coverage, special programs, school/business closings, and local talk shows.

BRYAN CURTIS

A S ONE OF THE LARGEST, MOST PROGRESSIVE, AND SUCCESSFUL insurance agencies in America, The Watson Group has provided individuals, families, and businesses with cost-effective and innovative solutions for their insurance and risk management needs since 1929. ❋ The firm has a well-earned reputation for honesty, integrity, and first-class customer service. The Watson Group takes

pride in the technical skills, professionalism, and caring attitude of its 90-person staff; the quality of its products and services; and its working relationship with nearly every major international, national, and regional insurance company.

Watson began as a typical property and casualty insurance agency providing basic protection and peace of mind to individuals and small-business owners throughout Greater Hartford. Over the years, the company's clients grew in number, size, and sophistication. Today, Watson is a diversified organization that writes more than $115 million per year in insurance premiums, and serves thousands of clients nationwide and overseas.

The key to Watson's transition from a small, local insurance agency to one of the top 150 agencies in the nation has been its ability to respond to the changing needs and demands of its clients. In 1961, the company established a separate Life, Employee Benefit, and Financial Services Division to help clients deal with the rapidly escalating costs of health care and related fringe benefit programs. Today, this division ranks among the largest operations of its kind in Connecticut and serves clients throughout the United States.

In 1967, Watson was one of the first insurance agencies in Connecticut to create a separate claims department to act as a liaison between its clients and insurance companies. Watson's highly trained staff of claim specialists seeks to minimize the frequency and severity of claims, and works diligently to ensure that all claims are settled promptly and fairly.

In 1981, Watson established its Professional Insurance Division to focus more attention on the unique needs of its many professional clients. The company has worked hard to earn the trust of this group, and now insures more than 2,000 Connecticut-based physicians and attorneys.

In 1983, Watson created a separate Bond Department to serve the surety needs of its many contractor clients. The firm now represents virtually every major surety company, and provides its clients with competitive rates, favorable terms, and the maximum capacity available in the marketplace.

Watson established its Sponsored Markets Division in 1988 to provide quality personal insurance products at discounted prices to members of associations, credit unions, and employer groups. This unique operation has enjoyed great success and now has a number of high-profile clients throughout the Northeast.

Watson most recently created its Captive Insurance Division to

assist those clients who require coverage, claims, and loss control services not readily available in the traditional marketplace. This operation is expected to experience significant growth over the next several years, as more and more companies seek alternative means of risk transfer and greater control of their long-term cost for insurance.

Looking toward the future, Watson is well positioned to continue its long-standing tradition of providing the highest level of service amid an environment of uncompromised professionalism. The company truly understands the importance of being on the forefront of change and the need to bring unparalleled value to its every relationship.

THE WATSON GROUP BOARD OF DIRECTORS: (CLOCKWISE FROM TOP LEFT) F. WILLIAM BARTON, VICE PRESIDENT; ALAN S. CURRIE, SENIOR VICE PRESIDENT; WILLIAM P. WITTMAN, VICE PRESIDENT; MICHAEL E. WATTS, SENIOR VICE PRESIDENT; THOMAS A. WILLSEY, PRESIDENT; AND PETER E. PETERSON, EXECUTIVE VICE PRESIDENT

TODAY, THE WATSON GROUP IS A DIVERSIFIED INSURANCE AGENCY THAT WRITES MORE THAN $115 MILLION PER YEAR IN INSURANCE PREMIUMS, AND SERVES THOUSANDS OF CLIENTS NATIONWIDE AND OVERSEAS.

Saint Joseph College

IN 1932, THE SISTERS OF MERCY OF CONNECTICUT HAD AN IDEA to establish the first liberal arts college for women in the Hartford area. It wasn't the best time for such a bold notion, considering the harsh economic times of the Great Depression and society's limited expectations of women. Led by Founding Dean Sister M. Rosa McDonough and bolstered by their fervent Catholic faith, they persisted and prevailed.

That same year, Saint Joseph College opened its doors to 63 women.

Today, the mission of the West Hartford college remains the same: to provide a rigorous liberal arts education, to promote the growth of the whole person, and to encourage ethical values, personal integrity, and a sense of societal responsibility. The premier four-year women's college in Connecticut, Saint Joseph is regularly cited by *U.S. News & World Report* as a top tier regional university and among the schools offering the best value.

WITH MATURE TREES, SPACIOUS LAWNS, AND RED BRICK GEORGIAN ARCHITECTURE, SAINT JOSEPH COLLEGE PERSONIFIES THE QUINTESSENTIAL NEW ENGLAND COLLEGE.

Education Based on Values

The college is recognized for its values-based education, including 30 undergraduate programs in edu-

◄ TOM WATSON

BECAUSE SAINT JOSEPH COLLEGE IS FOCUSED ON TEACHING, NOT RESEARCH, STUDENTS AND PROFESSORS ALIKE BENEFIT FROM A 12-TO-1 STUDENT-FACULTY RATIO AND AN AVERAGE CLASS SIZE OF 20 STUDENTS.

cation, nursing, human services, the humanities, and the sciences. Saint Joseph is one of only three colleges in Connecticut to offer combined preschool and elementary school teacher certification. The college also offers a master of arts degree, a master of science degree, and sixth year certificate programs, as well as prelaw and premed.

Although its Weekend College and Graduate School have been coeducational since the mid-1980s, Saint Joseph College is committed to remaining a women's college, noting that among the women listed in *Who's Who in America*, women's college graduates outnumber their counterparts from coed colleges 2-to-1. Total enrollment of the Women's College, Weekend College, and Graduate School exceeds 2,500 students. Most are Connecticut residents, more than half from Greater Hartford.

Saint Joseph College is both academically challenging and personally nurturing. Professors are recognized experts in their fields: Nearly 90 percent of them have Ph.D.'s or terminal degrees and five are Fulbright Scholars. Because the college is focused on teaching, not research, students and professors alike benefit from a 12-to-1 student-faculty ratio and an average class size of 20 students.

Focusing on Arts, Humanities, and Technology

With mature trees, spacious lawns, and red brick Georgian architecture, Saint Joseph College personifies the quintessential New England college. This is due to the school's adherence to the original 1935 blueprint developed by the Olmsted brothers, who also designed New York City's Central Park and Hartford's Bushnell Park.

The newest facility on the 84-acre campus is the Carol Autorino Center for the Arts and Humanities, a fittingly beautiful setting for a strong liberal arts tradition. While the building's wings face the campus center, the sides facing Asylum Avenue use a generous amount of glass to provide a window from the community into the college campus.

Students and area residents can enjoy musical and dramatic presentations and lectures in the arts center's 400-seat auditorium, as well as having access to its meeting and lecture rooms, art galleries, outdoor sculpture gallery, and bistro. Music practice rooms, seminar rooms, and a language laboratory support arts and humanities studies.

Keeping pace with the changes in society, the college recently opened the Information Technology Network Center. With both PC and Macintosh capabilities, the resource

center provides classrooms for computer science and mathematics.

Outside the classroom, students can pursue athletic interests, and the school's intercollegiate teams keep the competitive spirit alive. The Blue Jays have won Greater Northeast Athletic Conference championships in volleyball (in 1996, 1997, and 1998), basketball (in 1997 and 1998), and tennis (in 1999).

Serving Children with Special Needs

Saint Joseph College instills in its students the values of the Sisters of Mercy that include community outreach. More than 85 percent of Saint Joseph College students participate in the community, bettering society and themselves at the Trust House learning center for disadvantaged families, on Habitat for Humanity projects, and with other causes. Saint Joseph College itself fulfills its societal responsibility through exceptional services for children.

Soon after the college's founding, the Sisters of Mercy turned their attention to young children and designed a pioneering program to nurture the individuality of each child. In 1936, they established The School for Young Children, one of the first early childhood education centers in the state. Today, The School for Young Children—designated a Model Lab School by the Connecticut State Department of Education—has a long waiting list.

In 1999, The School for Young Children moved off campus into a state-of-the-art educational center

just a block from the college. Saint Joseph College renovated the former public school building with public and private funds, and leases it for $1 a year.

Besides providing quality education to preschoolers and kindergartners, The School for Young Children offers student teaching and classroom observation opportunities for Saint Joseph College students of early childhood education. It was one of the first laboratory sites in the nation designed for preschool teacher training.

On campus, The Gengras Center has served children with special needs since the 1960s. Students from elementary school through

age 18 attend the center from 48 surrounding towns. The center also functions as a laboratory for college students studying special education, psychology, and social work.

From its birth in the dark years of the depression to the promising beginning of the millennium, Saint Joseph College has grown with the times, while remaining true to the vision of its founding Sisters of Mercy of Connecticut. It has provided thousands of women with a superior education that encourages strong ethical values, personal integrity, and a sense of responsibility to societal needs.

THE COLLEGE IS RECOGNIZED FOR ITS VALUES-BASED EDUCATION, WHICH INCLUDES 30 UNDERGRADUATE PROGRAMS IN EDUCATION, NURSING, HUMAN SERVICES, THE HUMANITIES, AND THE SCIENCES.

SAINT JOSEPH COLLEGE IS BOTH ACADEMICALLY CHALLENGING AND PERSONALLY NURTURING.

Jeter, Cook & Jepson Architects, Inc.

{ **T**HE MELDING OF OLD AND NEW TYPIFIES THE EXEMPLARY DESIGNS AND overall firm vision that have distinguished Jeter, Cook & Jepson Architects, Inc. (JCJ) as a leader in the design profession. As the oldest architectural firm in the Hartford area, JCJ has completed 5,000 building projects since 1936, earning numerous regional and national awards for its innovative work. The firm is known for the diversity of its projects, and its }

educational, health care, hospitality/entertainment, government, and corporate facilities are designed with an optimal balance of aesthetic, functional, and financial considerations.

Recent area projects include the $1 billion expansion to Foxwoods Resort Casino, the most successful casino in the Western Hemisphere; LEGO's North American Headquarters and Creative Learning Center in Enfield and its Imagination Center in Minnesota's Mall of America; the State of Connecticut's Superior Courthouses in Middletown and Waterbury; and the University of

Connecticut's new downtown Waterbury Campus.

Clients Come First

JCJ has been justifiably honored by professional accolades, but it strives to earn its clients' satisfaction above all else. With a staff of more than 90 professionals, it is the largest architectural firm in the Hartford area, yet its personalized approach is more typical of smaller firms. JCJ's breadth of services is characteristic of much larger firms; by offering comprehensive planning, architectural, interior design, and graphic design services,

JCJ can take a client from site selection to a well-coordinated move-in. Ranked by *Engineering News Record* as the nation's 53rd-largest architectural firm, JCJ recognizes that teamwork and communication—within the firm and between its clients—are essential to success.

Serving Hartford for Six Decades

The firm's commitment to rejuvenating the city of Hartford is clear. JCJ is the managing architect for the $100 million Learning Corridor, an ambitious educational facilities

THE PROJECTS OF JETER, COOK & JEPSON ARCHITECTS, INC. (JCJ)— SUCH AS 100 PEARL STREET (RIGHT) AND CITYPLACE (LEFT)—DOT THE SKYLINE AND NEIGHBORHOODS OF HARTFORD.

AL FERREIRA

NICK WHEELER

JCJ's RENOVATION OF THE SAXE
MIDDLE SCHOOL (LEFT) AND DESIGN
OF WILBERT SNOW ELEMENTARY
SCHOOL (RIGHT) EARNED THE FIRM
NATIONAL ACCLAIM.

and neighborhood revitalization plan for the Frog Hollow neighborhood, adjacent to Trinity College.

In addition to this, JCJ is also completing a comprehensive facility study of Hartford's 35 public schools. The firm's projects dot the city's skyline and neighborhoods, including CityPlace II, 100 Pearl Street, the Learning Corridor, revitalization of Constitution Plaza, Coltsville Heritage Park, and Riverfront Recapture's treasured boathouse along the shore of the Connecticut River.

Known for strong management since its founding, JCJ has prepared a new generation of leadership. In January 2000, S. Edward Jeter, AIA, son of the founder, was named chairman; David Jepson, FAIA, was named chief executive officer; and Peter Stevens was named president. Along with an exemplary management team and talented staff, Jeter, Cook & Jepson Architects, Inc. will continue to retain a solid presence in Hartford, while applying the experience gained over the course of six decades of success to projects throughout the United States and abroad.

THE AWARD-WINNING NEW
MIDDLETOWN POLICE HEADQUAR-
TERS EXEMPLIFIES JCJ'S ABILITY TO
BRING A PROJECT FROM SITE SELEC-
TION AND PLANNING THROUGH
DESIGN AND CONSTRUCTION (LEFT).

OTHER RECENT AREA PROJECTS
INCLUDE LEGO'S CREATIVE
LEARNING CENTER IN ENFIELD
AND THE $1 BILLION EXPANSION
TO FOXWOODS RESORT CASINO
(BOTTOM LEFT AND RIGHT).

Connecticut Magazine

{E}OR NEARLY 30 YEARS, *Connecticut Magazine* HAS SHOWCASED THE MANY wonders of the Constitution State, from lovely Long Island Sound to historic Windsor, and from the Cornwall Bridge in the northwestern hills to the stone walls and country roads in the east. While promoting the state, the magazine has not shied away from in-depth reporting on people, issues, and events, and has become a trusted resource.

Connecticut Magazine first hit newsstands in September 1971, having evolved from a publication called *Connecticut Circle*. From the start, the magazine has covered issues and events of importance to its readers, helping them get the most out of what the state has to offer.

Connecticut Magazine's variety of thought-provoking articles reflect the interests and lifestyles of its readers. The lively editorial mix includes an indispensable calendar of events, comprehensive dining-out listings and restaurant reviews, articles on economic and political issues, and features on trends and personalities, business, health, travel, and the arts.

With a paid circulation of more than 85,000, *Connecticut* serves 210,000 educated, affluent, and active readers. Subscribers have an average household income of $119,100 and an average net worth of $740,000. Some 84 percent are college graduates.

The magazine, headquartered in Trumbull, employs 29 people in its editorial, art, production, sales, marketing, circulation, and administrative departments. *Connecticut* has been part of the Journal Register Company (JRC) since September 1999. JRC is a NYSE company, owning both daily newspapers—

including the *New Haven Register*—and numerous nondaily publications.

Award-Winning Articles

Connecticut Magazine's thoughtful selection of state-based content includes in-depth articles, service-oriented features, and personality profiles. National honors have come from the City and Regional Magazine Association (CRMA), which awarded *Connecticut* with medals for excellence in reporting in 1993, 1998, and 2000.

Among the magazine's most memorable work was Charles Monagan's "Casualty Aetna," which took a hard look at the merger of Aetna Inc. and U.S. Healthcare. The story won the CRMA Gold Medal for Reporting in 1998. In 2000, CRMA awarded Karon Haller its medal for reporting for "State v. Lapointe," which investigated how state and national media handled a murder conviction.

Other notable *Connecticut* articles have included "When a Bank Leaves Town," by David Howard, which illustrated what happens when a local bank, a longtime pillar of the community, is bought by a larger, out-of-town bank. Tom Connor's "Gods & Monsters" asked why the Diocese of Bridgeport sent abusive priests to new parishes. In "Huskies Inc.," Terese Karmel showed the University of Connecticut's national champion men's and women's basketball teams to be moneymaking machines. In April 2000, Debra Judge Silber updated Andrew Marlatt's comprehensive and colorful report, "Surfin' Safari: The State's Top 50

THE MANAGEMENT TEAM OF *Connecticut Magazine* COMPRISES (STANDING, FROM LEFT) MICHAEL MIMS, PRESIDENT AND PUBLISHER; JOCELYN PAOLETTA, MARKETING AND PROMOTIONS MANAGER; MARISA DRAGONE, PRODUCTION DIRECTOR; CHARLES A. MONAGAN, EDITOR; (SEATED, FROM LEFT) JOAN BARROW, ART DIRECTOR; ROBIN SCHUBEL, ADVERTISING DIRECTOR; L. LEE HEALY, CIRCULATION CONSULTANT; AND BARBARA H. SIMON, GENERAL MANAGER.

Web Sites," which had been published two years earlier.

The magazine often includes profiles of people of interest to area residents, such as Dr. Henry Lee, Oksana Baiul, Don Imus, James Van Der Beek, Kathie Lee Gifford, Kevin Bacon, and Victor Borge.

Popular regular features include "The Connecticut 100," an annual listing of the state's largest public and private companies, as well as banks, insurance companies, and subsidiaries. Every two years, the magazine publishes "Rating the Towns," an exclusive ranking of Connecticut's 169 cities and towns based on local schools, crime, cost of living, local economy, leisure, and cultural outlets. Monthly columns include Gardening, Connecticut Travel, and First Look/Fashion, plus Elise Maclay's restaurant reviews, which have received silver and gold medals from CRMA.

Boosting Charity and Tourism

In 1998, the magazine launched an annual event, Best of Connecticut™, to celebrate the state's "bests" and to benefit a charity. In its first three years, the event raised more than $125,000 for the March of Dimes in Connecticut.

Best of Connecticut begins in March, when readers choose the best of the state in dozens of categories that run from apple pie and jazz band to TV weatherperson. Winners are announced in September. Three weeks later, a major event stems from the readers' choices, with a fashion show, food, casino fun, and musical entertainment provided by the winners and sponsors. Michael Mims, the magazine's president and publisher, says, "The celebration of so many Connecticut bests in a single evening is a living extension of our editorial mission. We are extremely proud that it supports such a worthy cause."

The magazine fosters tourism through its Connecticut Travel column and its innovative marketing partnerships as well. Mystic Coast and Country recognized these efforts with its 1999 Golden Pineapple Award.

New Chapters: The Internet and Custom Publishing

The magazine's informative Internet site, www.connecticutmag.com, offers feature stories, Rating the Towns, Connecticut 100, restaurant listings, and an archive of Elise Maclay's reviews, state golf courses, wedding sites and services, county maps, and more.

Besides publishing the magazine, *Connecticut Magazine* has considerable experience and expertise for custom-publishing projects. Among its commemorative publications and souvenir programs for major sports events is the *Canon GHO Tournament Magazine*, which *Connecticut* published from 1996 to 1998. The magazine also published *Down to Earth*, a compilation of Rea Lubar Duncan's gardening columns.

Entering its third decade, *Connecticut Magazine* continues to evolve, says Editor Charles Monagan. "With an especially active and educated readership, it's imperative that we stay on the cutting edge of city and regional magazines. As long as the people in Connecticut remain interested in their surroundings, in the events and issues that affect their lives, *Connecticut Magazine* will continue as a trusted resource for them."

THE MAGAZINE'S EDITORIAL MIX INCLUDES AN INDISPENSABLE CALENDAR OF EVENTS, COMPREHENSIVE DINING-OUT LISTINGS AND RESTAURANT REVIEWS, ARTICLES ON ECONOMIC AND POLITICAL ISSUES, AND FEATURES ON TRENDS AND PERSONALITIES, BUSINESS, HEALTH, TRAVEL, AND THE ARTS.

Hospital for Special Care

A t Hospital for Special Care (HSC), an exceptional staff of highly skilled medical professionals work together with one ultimate goal in mind—to rebuild lives. A private, not-for-profit institution located in New Britain, Hospital for Special Care opened as a teaching facility in 1941. ❁ Today, HSC is the leading rehabilitation and chronic disease facility in the region. The

hospital is accredited by both the Joint Commission on Accreditation of Healthcare Organizations (JCAHO) and CARF: The Rehabilitation Accreditation Commission. CARF accredited programs at HSC include comprehensive inpatient rehabilitation, inpatient brain injury programs, outpatient rehabilitation, and the outpatient work-injury rehabilitation program. Hospital for Special Care is affiliated with the University of Connecticut as a teaching hospital.

A Focus on Teamwork

The hospital's management model brings together doctors, nurses, therapists, administrators, and other health care professionals working in teams to focus on specific patient needs. Patient-care teams work in centralized settings to maximize interaction and communication between caregivers, patients, and their families. To support the hospital's mission "to provide exemplary rehabilitation and continuing medical care with the active invol-

JOHN ATASHIAN

vement of our patients and their families," HSC is organized into three services: inpatient and outpatient rehabilitation, respiratory, and medically complex pediatrics.

Leading HSC's multidisciplinary approach to providing the highest quality of care is a staff physiatrist, a physician with a specialty in rehabilitation and physical medicine. In addition, a case manager coordinates care during a patient's hospital stay, serving as a patient

advocate and someone to whom the patient, family, and professional team can look for support and information.

HSC's rehabilitation services offer both inpatient and outpatient programs designed to help patients with complex orthopedic and neurological problems become as independent as possible. Staffed by an interdisciplinary team of professionals, including a cadre of highly skilled physical, occupational, speech, and recreation therapists, the hospital's rehabilitation unit provides programs for people needing acute rehabilitation due to serious illness or physical trauma; longer-term inpatient neurobehavioral and chronic care programs; and numerous outpatient services, from daylong, multitherapy sessions to hour-long sessions for chronic back pain. The unit also features a daily living apartment where patients and their families can simulate the home environment prior to their discharge.

The hospital's multilevel respiratory services treat individuals with serious breathing problems resulting from neuromuscular conditions, stroke, and pulmonary disease. To maximize the treatment of various conditions, HSC offers three levels of care: the Close Observation Unit, offering complex medical care for patients needing advanced technological

AL FERREIRA

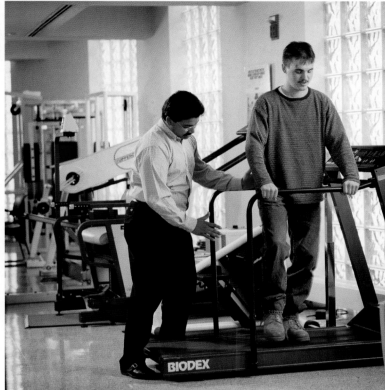

intervention; the Respiratory Care Unit—including the nation's largest unit for ventilator-dependent patients—for patients needing ventilator assistance on a 24-hour basis; and the Respiratory Step Down Unit, for people requiring artificial ventilation on a less intensive basis. Respiratory services also include a nationally recognized regional weaning center, where patients transition from long-term mechanical ventilation toward regaining their independence.

Hospital for Special Care's pediatric services offer care for children with severe and complex health problems, including those who are technology dependent. The unit is comprised of a dedicated team of experts focusing solely on the requirements of the hospital's youngest patients. Treatment on the pediatric unit is highly individualized, with lengths of stay ranging from a few days to more than a year. The goal for every child—regardless of his or her length of stay or the complexity of the child's illness—is to get back home.

Aquatic Rehabilitation Center

In recognition of the benefits of aquatic exercise and aquatic therapy, Hospital for Special Care opened a state-of-the-art Aquatic Rehabilitation Center on the hospital grounds. The center features two wheelchair-accessible pools,

a warm-water pool for aquatic therapy, and a cooler pool for fitness and athletic training. The Aquatic Rehabilitation Center also features a modern fitness center complete with cardiovascular and strength-training equipment that currently serves people of all abilities, including wheelchair athletes.

Sports and Fitness

Hospital for Special Care's commitment to sports and fitness extends far beyond the hospital grounds. For example, HSC is the managing sponsor of the Cruisers, a team of young, physically disabled Connecticut athletes who compete locally, regionally, and nationally in wheelchair track-and-field competitions, where many Cruisers have set several national records. Through

Special Care's Ivan Lendl Junior Wheelchair Sports Camp—the first and only one of its kind on the East Coast—world-class disabled athletes provide campers with instruction in tennis, swimming, basketball, and track and field at no cost, thanks to the fundraising success of Special Care's Annual Ivan Lendl Golf Tournament.

HSC also sponsors its own wheelchair basketball team, as well as the USA Women's Wheelchair Basketball team. Other sports programs include the HSC Wave swim team, Skiers Unlimited, and numerous adapted sports programs, clinics, conferences, and symposiums, all part of an effort to champion the cause of the disabled athlete through education, information, and advocacy.

A Continuum of Care

As part of its continuum of care, Hospital for Special Care provides other facilities and programs for its patients and the community at large, including Brittany Farms Health Center, a 284-bed, state-of-the-art health care facility specializing in subacute rehabilitation and long-term care; Special Care Holistic Wellness Connection, a facility that merges traditional and nontraditional medicines; neighborhood residences for lower- to middle-income older adults with physical disabilities; and Special Care Dental Services, a dental program for Medicaid-eligible children and adolescents. HSC also offers support groups for patients and families affected by arthritis, Guillain-Barré syndrome, stroke, head injury, Parkinson's disease, and pulmonary conditions.

THE HOSPITAL'S MANAGEMENT MODEL BRINGS TOGETHER DOCTORS, NURSES, THERAPISTS, ADMINISTRATORS, AND OTHER HEALTH CARE PROFESSIONALS WORKING IN TEAMS TO FOCUS ON SPECIFIC PATIENT NEEDS.

THE MISSION OF HSC IS "TO PROVIDE EXEMPLARY REHABILITATION AND CONTINUING MEDICAL CARE WITH THE ACTIVE INVOLVEMENT OF OUR PATIENTS AND THEIR FAMILIES."

Moore Medical
Corporation

A
T THE TYPICAL WORKPLACE, A LOOK IN THE FIRST AID KIT WILL
unveil some Moore Medical products among its contents. Check-
ing the ambulances that serve any town will reveal more Moore
Medical-supplied products. In addition, a visit to the podiatrist
will involve the treatment of patients with an instrument, bandage,
or solution distributed by The Supply Experts™ at Moore Medical.

EACH YEAR, DEPUTY DIRECTOR OF
NEW BRITAIN EMS EDWARD COSTA
DRIVES AN AMBULANCE TO MOORE
MEDICAL'S HEADQUARTERS TO CON-
DUCT AN ON-SITE TRAINING SESSION
FOR CUSTOMER REPRESENTATIVES.

Based in New Britain, Moore Medical is one of the leading distributors of medical and surgical supplies, personal-protection equipment, and basic office supplies to doctors, emergency medical services, pharmacies, continuing care facilities, and consumers.

Over the course of some 50 years, the company has grown from modest roots in the back room of the Axelrod Pharmacy in downtown New Britain. Now, Moore Medical stands at the forefront of the e-commerce revolution in the medical supplies field. In July 1998, the company launched its Web site—mooremedical.com—which features on-line ordering and live chat with a Moore representative. The company's full catalog of products is represented on-line as well.

Statistics have shown the health care industry slow to embrace the Internet for commerce. Moore is working aggressively to change that by making it easy and convenient for health care providers to buy on-line. Yet, the company and its unparalleled standards of service remain rooted in every customer service professional, order filler, and sales representative.

"We're not just trying to throw everything on the Web," says Linda Autore, president and CEO of Moore Medical Corporation. "Some of our people have a propensity to move to the Web. Our sales figures show that there are people buying on-line in 'step levels' to get comfortable with it."

While retaining its off-line relationships, Moore Medical plans to offer the best of both worlds to its 100,000 health care professional customer base.

Although mooremedical.com has already shown itself to be a portal for health care information and an easy-ordering site for many health care professionals, Moore plans to keep its phone, fax, conventional mail, and in-person sales forces as strong as ever. Through partnerships with on-line powerhouses such as MERGInet.com and Podiatry Online, Moore Medical now reaches almost 40,000 medical professionals on-line.

A Wide Selection of Products

Today, Moore Medical maintains one of the most complete selections of emergency medical products and related product lines in the industry, offering approximately 10,000 products, including gauze and wound dressings, IV solutions, ointments, crutches, and diagnostic and test equipment.

Moore Medical is now known as

The Supply Experts™ to customers as diverse as office-based and medical specialty physicians, group practices, clinics, industrial plants, emergency medical services (EMS) squads, schools, universities, and correctional institutions, as well as federal, state, and local governments. The company offers brand-name products made by some of the leading names in medical supply, including Johnson & Johnson, Textilease Medique, and Miltex, along with Moore Medical's own high-quality, economical brand.

The people who are Moore Medical are empowered by more than corporate buzzwords and rallies. A new, state-of-the-art business and customer service system gives employees instant and consistent product, financial, and account information for every customer. This enables the most informed representatives in the industry to offer custom-tailored service to everyone who deals with Moore Medical.

"We believe we empower health care professionals—those who save lives and improve wellness—with the tools they need: pharmaceuticals, supplies, and instruments," Autore says.

Although its focus is on the health care practitioner market, Moore Medical continues to sell a significant amount of prescription drugs to registered and fully licensed customers.

Passionate about Customer Service

Moore Medical strives to find better ways to serve its diverse customers—from individual practitioners to emergency service providers to large industrial site medical centers.

Knowing customers appreciate on-time, accurate deliveries, Moore Medical maintains one of the largest inventories in the business, as well as a strong infrastructure of regional distribution centers in New Britain; Visalia; Jacksonville, Florida; and Lemont, Illinois.

More than half of Moore Medical's employees work in marketing, sales, and customer relations, offering strong evidence of the company's customer-focused philosophy. The firm's highly trained Customer Support Center representatives are knowledgeable, efficient, and friendly, and they care about each and every customer who calls.

Moore Medical's employees are health specialty experts. For example, certified emergency medical technicians work in the Emergency Medical Services Unit, and telephone sales representatives specialize in one or more customer groups so they can provide a range of specific product and industry expertise.

"Knowledge of our customers' practice and business operations, as well as the markets they represent, is a performance objective," says Autore. "Frequent discussions with our customers, including on-site requirement visits and meetings with members of our Customer Council keep us close to their changing needs. We are pleased that our customers consistently rate us superior in value and responsiveness, and we continually raise our own expectations for performance in service measurements."

Forging Strong Bonds with Customers

Moore Medical enjoys forming strong relationships with its customers to help them manage their businesses more efficiently. The company's Web site keeps up on industry competition and trends

within its customer areas, offers continuing education to keep customers up to date in their professions, recommends books, and provides immediate responses to customer inquiries.

The relationship between Moore Medical and New Britain Emergency Medical Services, a customer since 1991, is an example of the company's unusual bond with its customers. New Britain EMS is a nonprofit organization that provides 911 emergency medical services, responding to approximately 10,000 calls a year at the paramedical level. Each year, Deputy Director Edward Costa drives an ambulance to Moore Medical's headquarters and conducts an on-site training session for customer representatives.

"We go through the ambulance, tell them about the EMS system, and explain the levels of certifications and available licenses," Costa explains. "They learn the difference between emergency medical technicians and paramedics, as well as the various types of products they order. We also explain regional and state differences regarding transport times to reach hospitals. With all of this information, they

"WE ARE PLEASED THAT OUR CUSTOMERS CONSISTENTLY RATE US SUPERIOR IN VALUE AND RESPONSIVENESS, AND WE CONTINUALLY RAISE OUR OWN EXPECTATIONS FOR PERFORMANCE IN SERVICE MEASUREMENTS," SAYS LINDA AUTORE, PRESIDENT AND CEO OF MOORE MEDICAL CORPORATION.

have a much better understanding of their EMS customers."

Over the years, New Britain EMS employees have posed for photos for Moore Medical's product catalogs, and in return, the company has helped New Britain EMS produce fund-raising brochures. "Moore Medical provides the highest level of quality customer service 100 percent of the time," Costa says.

Central Connecticut State University (CCSU) has been a Moore Medical customer since 1993. President Richard Judd considers the company a partner. "Moore Medical goes well beyond filling our needs for medical equipment and supplies," Judd says. "We have forged a partnership that will expand the normal supplier relationship into helping us use equipment better and more intelligently. They go beyond the cutting edge to what I call the caring edge."

Moore Medical and CCSU have formed a top-notch advisory team of medical and training experts to serve as an outreach, expanding organizations' knowledge and use of medical equipment and supplies.

This partnership offers a cost benefit to the buyer in utilization, training, and in-depth knowledge of a particular medical device or item, and also links Moore Medical and CCSU in a collaborative way. Says Judd, "I do not know of similar organizations that have actively embraced such forward-thinking linkages."

Serving the Community

The Charter Oak Family Health Center, located in Hartford and a Moore Medical customer since 1992, serves as a member on Moore Medical's 11-member Customer Council Advisory Board. "By serving on the board, Moore allows us to share our professional experiences and suggestions to improve the products and services it provides to its customers," states Laurel Coleman, development director. "In turn, Moore Medical continues to supply us with the products we need, allowing our center to care for our patients and improve the lives we touch in the community," The center is community based, and focuses on providing high-quality, affordable health care services to those who are in need and who of-

ten are unable to afford such services.

As it fosters partnerships with customers, Moore Medical also develops strategic relationships with major manufacturers. This gives customers access to the latest products and information, as well as the benefit of the company's buying power.

With strong roots in the community, Moore Medical is considered one of New Britain's top employers, and the company and its staff contribute greatly to the vitality of central Connecticut. They support more than 50 organizations in the area, including the Connecticut Children's Medical Center, YMCA, American Diabetes Association, New Britain General Hospital, and Friendship Center.

Moore Medical has more than 50 years' experience in providing superior customer service, a strong reputation as medical supply experts, and a demonstrated ability to reinvent itself as markets change. To ensure continued success, the company is committed to improving every part of its operation and to meeting the unique needs of its specialized customer markets with its brand of service.

THE CHARTER OAK FAMILY HEALTH CENTER, LOCATED IN HARTFORD AND A MOORE MEDICAL CUSTOMER SINCE 1992, SERVES AS A MEMBER ON MOORE MEDICAL'S 11-MEMBER CUSTOMER COUNCIL ADVISORY BOARD.

ED UP WITH THE TRAFFIC AND CONGESTION OF THE NEW YORK AND Boston airports, New England travelers have opted for the alternative choice, Bradley International Airport. It is easily New England's most convenient major airport, both for its easy access to interstate highways and for its availability when freezing rain, snow, or fog closes larger facilities. ❋ As New England's second-largest airport, Bradley

International serves Hartford/ Springfield and western New England from Windsor Locks. Its 20 passenger airlines offer more than 300 flights daily to and from 80 popular destinations throughout the United States, Canada, and the Caribbean.

Expansion Endeavors

Built in 1941 as Windsor Locks Air Base, the facility was designated Bradley Field in 1942 by the War Department in honor of U.S. Army Air Corps Lieutenant Eugene Bradley, a young pilot from Oklahoma who died in a training accident while stationed at the base. During World War II, the airport was a major embarkation point for bombers headed for Europe and for the redeployment of airmen. It also served briefly as a prisoner of war camp for German soldiers. In 1947, the army returned the facility to the state, and in January 1948, Eastern Airlines became the first commercial carrier to operate from Connecticut's newest airport.

Thanks to its location, new carriers, and affordability, a record 6.3 million passengers used Bradley International in 1999, a 12 percent increase over the previous year. In 1999, *Airline International* called it the nation's sixth-fastest-growing airport. With major construction projects under way and increased competition among low-fare carriers, the airport expects double-digit growth to continue in the years ahead.

Bradley International's success is an economic boon to the tourism industry, businesses, and residents of Connecticut and western Massachusetts. By 2009, its financial impact is expected to reach $2.4 billion annually. To preserve this asset, the State of Connecticut, which owns and operates Bradley International, has begun an ambitious transformation with $200 million in expansion and improvements.

The plan includes demolition of aging Terminal B and construction of a new terminal with wider concourses, additional boarding gates, larger ticketing and baggage claim areas, and improved access roads. Completion is expected in 2003. The state also plans to construct a 3,500-space parking garage. The Sheraton Bradley Hotel, located on-site, also has plans for expansion.

Increasing Passenger Traffic

New, low-fare carriers have greatly enhanced Bradley's popularity since 1996, when Delta Express started service from the Hartford area to major destinations and introduced competitive pricing. In 1998, US Airways introduced MetroJet service, while Midwest Express and Shuttle America began serving Bradley International. On October 31, 1999, Bradley International became the largest airport in the

Northeast to attract Southwest Airlines, a legend among low-fare airlines. Almost immediately, every carrier at Bradley reported increased business. For the first time, December traffic at the airport exceeded 500,000 passengers. Another low-fare carrier, America West Airlines, began operating out of Bradley in 2000.

As with its thriving passenger business, Bradley International's location also makes it a popular cargo port, serving 11 cargo carriers. In 1997, UPS built its Northeast distribution center at the airfield, resulting in Bradley International's ranking as the 37th-largest cargo airport in North America.

Building on its successful past, recent expansion, and record business, Bradley International Airport hopes to become a transatlantic gateway, provide nonstop service to Europe, and expand nonstop service to cities in the western United States.

BRADLEY INTERNATIONAL AIRPORT—EASILY NEW ENGLAND'S MOST CONVENIENT MAJOR AIRPORT—SERVES HARTFORD/ SPRINGFIELD AND WESTERN NEW ENGLAND FROM WINDSOR LOCKS.

Hartford Office Supply

WHEN HARTFORD OFFICE SUPPLY OPENED AS A SMALL STORE-front in 1950, the company's shelves were stocked with a sparse assortment of postwar America's business tools—carbon paper, fountain pens, ink wells, mimeograph supplies, and desk blotters, as well as other simple items. Today, the company has offices in three states, and its

6,500-item inventory reflects the business needs of the 21st century. Diskettes, laser printers, ink-jet cartridges, and other computer-related products comprise more than 60 percent of the firm's stock. With annual sales exceeding $50 million, Hartford Office Supply has become the top distributor of office supplies in the Northeast.

A Family-Run National Leader

More than 5,000 local and regional companies throughout New England and Westchester County, New York, are active customers of Hartford Office Supply. As the firm has continued to meet the evolving needs of these companies for more than five decades, it has remained family owned and family run.

Company President Richard Kilpatrick Jr. is a son of Richard Kilpatrick, who founded the company with his partner, Everett Scanlon. Other second-generation family members active in the company are

the president's brothers, Robert and Kevin Kilpatrick, and Treasurer Robert Flannery, Scanlon's son.

The Hartford-based company is the fifth largest of the 6,000 independent office supply distributors in the United States. Before the advent of national superstore

chains, there were as many as 13,000 independent distributors.

Richard Kilpatrick Jr. sees advantages in being an independent supplier. "We're big enough to compete with the chains, but small enough to work with customers as their partners and to provide personal services such as dedicated customer service representatives and customized items," Kilpatrick says.

Custom preprinted requisition forms list a customer's standard supply products, which saves time and reduces errors and unnecessary expenses. Custom catalogs allow quick product identification, and answer frequently asked questions about products, ordering procedures, returns, and key contacts within the company.

Instead of listing confusing and misleading manufacturers' suggested retail prices or ordering codes, Hartford Office Supply catalogs clearly indicate wholesale net prices on every item, so customers know exactly what they are buying.

Using Technology to Serve Customers

Hartford Office Supply supplements its personal touch with technology, ensuring that superior service extends from the moment

LEADING HARTFORD OFFICE SUPPLY ARE (FROM LEFT) ROBERT FLANNERY, CHARLIE CLEARY, ROBERT KILPATRICK, AND RICHARD KILPATRICK JR.

ORDERS ARE PICKED, PACKED, AND DELIVERED NEXT DAY TO VIRTUALLY ANY LOCATION IN NEW ENGLAND ON HARTFORD OFFICE SUPPLY'S OWN FLEET OF TRUCKS.

to help customers save time and money. The cost of processing payments for invoices, for example, can be reduced by electronic storage media (CD, diskette, or EDI), departmental summary invoices, and electronic funds transfer. The company also will track historical usage and produce reports to help customers control their supply expenses.

The firm has three strategic locations. Most of its 200 employees, many from the city's neighborhoods, work at the headquarters and distribution center in Hartford. In Littleton, Massachusetts, and Johnston, Rhode Island, the company has sales offices, customer service staff, and warehouses. Deliveries from Hartford arrive in outlying offices by midnight for next-day delivery.

As it begins its sixth decade, Hartford Office Supply plans to grow throughout its northeastern marketplace by continuing to provide high-quality products at the lowest possible prices, next-day guaranteed delivery, and personalized service that is the best in the business.

a customer places an order, to guaranteed next-day delivery almost anywhere in New England. Understanding that every customer is different, the company has replaced a once paper-intensive ordering process with more efficient options: telephone, e-mail, fax, customized requisitions, and electronic data interchange (EDI), as well as the Internet.

Another ordering option is Hartford Office Supply's own InstaLink Plus (Ordway), which allows orders to be placed directly through the computer. The system provides access to a complete catalog of 23,000 items and up-to-date pricing information.

Hartford Office Supply's 200,000-square-foot distribution center on Capitol Avenue in Hartford is fully automated, with conveyor systems, gravity flow racks, "quick pick" bulk modules, carousels, and a sophisticated routing system. The center provides quick, efficient, and accurate processing of orders, and every order is quality inspected before shipping.

Kilpatrick says, "We have more than $5 million in inventory and a huge selection of brand-name products, but if an item happens to be out of stock, we will find it and still get it to the customer the next day. We can also accommodate emergencies and make same-day deliveries almost anywhere in our service area. It is easy to return items, too.

We include an authorization form with every order and will pick up any returns while making routine deliveries. In everything we do, we strive to exceed customers' expectations. That was true when my father started the business, and it is true today."

Helping Customers Reduce Expenses

Customers are well served by Hartford Office Supply's 45 sales representatives, each with more than 10 years of experience on average. They work with customers as partners to reduce costs, increase productivity, save time, and simplify ordering.

Hartford Office Supply offers a number of innovative options

American Airlines, Inc.

HARTFORD HAS BEEN CONSIDERED A HOME AWAY FROM HOME FOR American Airlines, Inc. since its service to the area began in 1952 with flights to LaGuardia Airport in New York City. In the early 1960s, American flew as many as 55 jets per day from Hartford's Bradley Airport to destinations like New York's LaGuardia and JFK airports, Chicago, Dallas, Nashville, and Los Angeles.

By the mid-1980s, American had increased its local services with regular flights to San Juan, Puerto Rico; Miami; Dallas/Fort Worth; Chicago; Nashville; and Raleigh/ Durham, and its regional partner, American Eagle, was also serving LaGuardia and JFK. Today, 13 American Airline jets and four Eagles fly from Hartford to JFK every day, and American is the only carrier at Bradley with daily service to Dallas, Los Angeles, Miami, and San Juan.

American demonstrated its commitment to the area by opening its Eastern Reservations Office on Main Street in Hartford in 1976. Today, the airline employs some 900 people in the capital city, serving customers throughout the United States.

AMERICAN AIRLINES, INC. DEMONSTRATED ITS COMMITMENT TO THE HARTFORD AREA BY OPENING ITS EASTERN RESERVATIONS OFFICE IN THE CITY IN 1976. TODAY, THE AIRLINE EMPLOYS SOME 900 PEOPLE IN THE CAPITAL CITY, SERVING CUSTOMERS THROUGHOUT THE UNITED STATES.

A Leader Emerges

Twenty-six years before American's arrival in Hartford, Charles A. Lindbergh took off from Chicago for St. Louis with a single bag of mail, thus inaugurating the first regularly scheduled flight for what would later become American Airlines.

Lindbergh was the chief pilot for Robertson Aircraft Corporation of Missouri, one of nearly 80 companies that merged in 1934 to become American Airlines. In the decades since that merger, American has faced and met the challenges of the changing airline industry, and become a global leader in the process.

Originally headquartered in New York, American moved to the Dallas/Fort Worth area in 1979, and began developing its first hub at Dallas/Fort Worth International Airport two years later. In the years following the 1978 deregulation of the U.S. airline industry, American expanded greatly.

Today, American Airlines and American Eagle operate a fleet of more than 850 aircraft, employ more than 102,000 people, serve nearly 300 markets, and complete more than 4,000 daily flights throughout the world.

An Industry Pioneer

Throughout its history, American Airlines has led the industry with innovative ideas and programs. In 1933, American was the first airline to introduce flight attendants and, the following year, originated an air traffic control system that was later adopted by all airlines and administered by the U.S. government. A mid-1930s collaboration with the Douglas Air-

craft Company resulted in the development of the DC-3, one of the most famous commercial airplanes ever built. By 1937, American celebrated carrying its one-millionth passenger.

In 1953, American flew the first nonstop transcontinental route from Los Angeles to New York with the Douglas DC-7, and six years later, the airline was the first to upgrade this route with the much faster Boeing 707. As those jets came on line, American introduced SABRE, the world's first computer reservations system, which today is used by thousands of travel agents in more than 70 countries.

In 1981, the AAdvantage Frequent Flyer Program was introduced, marking a revolutionary new way to attract and retain customers, and in 1992, the Alliance Maintenance and Engineering Base was opened, the first state-of-the-art airline maintenance facility to be built in the United States in more than 20 years.

With the oneworld™ product, which includes partnerships between American Airlines and seven other carriers, including Finnair and Iberia, American can provide service to more than 655 destinations in more than 135 countries. The product also includes frequent flyer recognition between the carriers and more seamless transactions at the ticket counter.

A Promising Future

American's pioneering tradition continues as it charts new courses in Internet technology. As of 1996, customers could book travel on-line via American's AAccess page, and by the following year, more than 1 million customers were receiving e-mail notices of discount fares through the Net SAAver program.

In addition, American is expanding the breadth and depth of its international network. In 1998, the airline received permission to begin additional service to Japan, thereby strengthening its presence in the Pacific Rim. American also has announced code-sharing partnerships with several Latin American carriers and an agreement with Swissair/Sabena that will considerably enhance its international system.

A large part of American's long-range plans revolves around its more than 20-year partnership with Boeing. In 1998, American began acquiring several new 767s, and a year later, added super-long-range 777s to its fleet. By 2002, American will have added more than 150 new aircraft to its system, ensuring that the airline will continue to operate the youngest and most advanced fleet in the industry.

Serving the Community

Striving to be something special in the air and on the ground, American makes it a priority to participate in

programs that positively affect every community it serves. In the Hartford area, the airline and its employees have supported worthwhile causes and programs such as the Cystic Fibrosis Foundation, Susan G. Komen Breast Cancer Foundation, United Negro College Fund, and United Way. In addition to sponsoring the Hartford Marathon and

the Greater Hartford Open, the airline supports the football and basketball programs at the University of Connecticut.

From the days of Lindbergh's mail route to today's increasingly global and technologically driven industry, one trend is clear: American Airlines has been, and will continue to be, a leader in its field.

TODAY, AMERICAN AIRLINES AND AMERICAN EAGLE OPERATE A FLEET OF MORE THAN 850 AIRCRAFT, EMPLOY MORE THAN 102,000 PEOPLE, SERVE NEARLY 300 MARKETS, AND COMPLETE MORE THAN 4,000 DAILY FLIGHTS THROUGHOUT THE WORLD.

WVIT-NBC 30

I
N THE NEWS BUSINESS, REPORTERS WHO KNOW AND UNDERSTAND THE PEOPLE and the community get the story first, and they get it right. When Connecticut residents want television news coverage that is truly "live, local, and late-breaking," they turn the dial to Hartford's first television station, NBC 30. ❊ As the home of the state's most experienced reporting team, NBC 30 is a news powerhouse. Several reporters have been with the station

for decades. Tom Monahan signed on in 1965, while Lew Brown joined in 1979, Anchor Joanne Nesti followed in 1981, and Chief Meteorologist Brad Field came to the station in 1983. That wealth of experience shows in the ratings. In 1999, NBC 30's reporters, anchors, and technicians produced Connecticut's most-watched news programs, airing at 5 a.m. and 11 p.m.

More Than 50 Years of Success

For nearly 50 years, NBC 30 has informed, entertained, and moved millions of Connecticut residents. Julian Gross, owner of radio station WKNB, founded NBC 30 in 1953 and served as its general manager for several years. While its headquarters was under construction, the station broadcast from its transmitter site on Rattlesnake Mountain in Farmington. After a year, NBC 30 moved its operations into a new building in West Hartford that accommodated both the radio station and the television sta-

tion. The small facility, with three levels, no elevators, and a studio in the center, facilitated teamwork and increased NBC 30's ability to go on air quickly. The new station also had a unique feature—a large garage door that enabled a live broadcast of the Hartford Auto Show by driving cars into the studio.

Connecticut residents embraced the new television station, which broadcast in black and white, with enthusiasm, and the station was extremely popular from the beginning. In 1955, for instance, Tex Pavel's cowboy-style show for children had a three-and-a-half year waiting list.

As with many long-running businesses, the local television station has had several owners. In 1956, Gross kept the radio station and sold the TV station to the National Broadcasting Company (NBC), which owned and operated it for many years with the call letters of WNBC. The station was known as WHNB from 1960 until

1978, when Viacom assumed ownership and changed the call letters to WVIT. Since 1997, NBC has owned and operated the station, which still is known as WVIT. Through this partnership, WVIT, with NBC and its sister stations, shares personnel and equipment as well as information, which significantly enhances the capabilities of NBC 30.

In addition to being Hartford's first television station, NBC 30 boasts several other firsts. In 1957, it became the first color TV station in Connecticut. The station hired New England's first female weatherperson, Cavell Jobert, in 1953; she continued working at the station until 1968. When Jim Moore joined the station in the 1960s, he was Connecticut's first African-American television reporter.

Caring for the Community

A long wall in the station displays many awards and plaques that reflect the quality of NBC 30's

NBC 30 PERSONALITIES (FROM LEFT) JANET PECKINPAUGH, GERRY BROOKS, AND JOANNE NESTI CONSISTENTLY DELIVER LIVE, LOCAL, LATE-BREAKING NEWS.

programming. In 1989, the station won a Public Service Emmy for "Cocaine Babies." In 1999, the station received an Associated Press Broadcaster's Association Recognition award and a United Press International award for "Breaking the Cycle," a program examining teen pregnancy, presented by the Hartford Action Plan on Infant Health, the City of Hartford, and the Hartford Public Schools. NBC 30 has also been honored by Sigma Delta Chi and received several Best News Program awards from *Hartford Advocate* readers.

The NBC 30 news staff has a long-standing practice of working to improve its community. Perhaps its shining hour occurred early in its history, in August 1955, when the station mounted an around-the-clock telethon to help thousands of local residents made homeless by a devastating flood. Celebrities such as Rudy Vallee, Bob Hope, and Bert Parks all pitched in.

In more recent years, NBC 30 has cosponsored Button Up Connecticut, which provides coats for Connecticut's needy; Joy of Sharing, which collects new toys for the holidays; the Special Olympics; and many other activities. Organizations such as the March of Dimes WalkAmerica, FoodShare,

IN ADDITION TO BEING HARTFORD'S FIRST TELEVISION STATION, NBC 30 BOASTS SEVERAL OTHER FIRSTS. IN 1957, IT BECAME THE FIRST COLOR TV STATION IN CONNECTICUT.

THE STATION WAS KNOWN AS WHNB FROM 1960 UNTIL 1978, WHEN VIACOM ASSUMED OWNERSHIP AND CHANGED THE CALL LETTERS TO WVIT.

Air Force Recruiting, American Lung Association, American Diabetes Association, and Arthritis Foundation have recognized the station's goodwill.

While NBC 30 reflects on the richness of its past, the station continues to celebrate and embrace the future with creative enterprise. NBC 30's desire to serve its community of viewers has spawned a series of innovative Internet projects both on air and on-line. Most notably, on April 9, 2000, NBC 30 produced a live Web cast of the UConn Women's Basketball Team's NCAA victory parade in Hartford. NBC 30 was the first station in Connecticut to use live, streaming video in order

to deliver a local community event to viewers. Thousands of cyber viewers—some as far away as California and Florida—logged on to view the parade on NBC30.com.

Technological advances such as digital television and the Internet undoubtedly will revolutionize television news reporting. There will be new ways to access information, along with improved picture and sound quality. Whatever the changes, NBC 30 will remain an important source of information for the people of Connecticut. Its viewers can bank on the station's traditions of "live, local, and late-breaking" news coverage and community service for decades to come.

Loctite Corporation

D R. VERNON KRIEBLE, A RETIRED TRINITY COLLEGE PROFESSOR of chemistry, often tinkered in the basement of his Hartford home. One day in 1953, his son Robert—also a Ph.D. chemist—presented him with a challenge that was considered unsolvable: How could they keep anaerobic permafil from hardening before its time? Krieble knew the sealant could be useful for applications like nuts and bolts,

but he did not know how to store the substance.

The professor set to work in his laboratory and soon discovered a solution—a cure inhibition system for the unique liquid bonding resin that hardened in the absence of air. Krieble founded the American Sealants Company to produce his invention, which his wife, Nancy, named Loctite because it locked nuts and bolts tight. In 1956, the company was renamed Loctite Corporation in honor of its original product.

For all his imagination, it is unlikely that Krieble could have envisioned that his basement invention would spawn a worldwide corporation with sales surpassing $1 billion at the millennium's end.

Growth through Innovation

As additional adhesives, sealants, and coatings were developed, sales began to skyrocket. The company recorded nearly $2 million in sales and $220,000 in net income after its first decade. Loctite merged with International Sealants in 1970, and acquired the firm's overseas distributors. By 1975, sales had reached $67 million, and Loctite's stock was soon listed on the New York Stock Exchange.

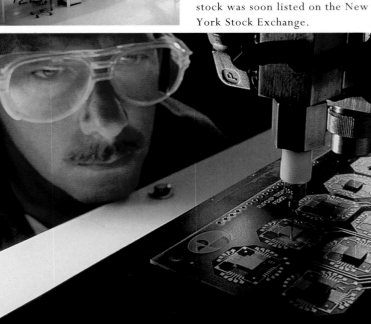

Acquisitions followed, as research and development opened up the possibilities of new markets. Permatex Company and Woodhill Chemical Sales Company were a few of Loctite's acquisitions. In 1997, the company became a division of Henkel KGaA, a global market leader in specialty chemicals and consumer products, headquartered in Germany.

Since the beginning, the company has grown through product innovation. Each year, Loctite invests nearly $30 million in new product development. Loctite engineers and chemists—including more chemistry Ph.D.'s than are found at most universities—are hard at work in research laboratories around the world.

Loctite's product development experts team up with sales engineers, who respond with imagination when clients ask them to develop better methods of manufacturing products. By working closely with clients, Loctite has carved itself a niche in the industry, finding unique solutions through science and ingenuity.

Loctite Products Are Everywhere

Today, the little company that began with one product has more than 1,000 and conducts business in more than 80 countries. Loctite has become a worldwide leader in its field, offering diversified contri-

butions to daily life. Its products are used to make a vast array of appliances, machines, and electronic equipment—from automobiles, computers, CD players, and VCRs to cameras, medical devices, and hearing aids.

For example, Loctite developed Indermil, a first-of-its-kind medical adhesive, to replace staples or sutures to close wounds. The sterilized adhesive lets wounds heal safely, with improved comfort for the patient.

Nearly every car that rolls off an American or Canadian assembly line has at least one Loctite application, from gasketing and threadlockers to bonding parts in every part of the vehicle—from the engine to the transmission, and from the interior to the exterior.

For digital versatile disc (DVD) manufacturers, which distribute audio, video, and computer products, Loctite developed light-curing adhesives that transform the DVD-substrate bonding phase into an easier, faster, and more cost-efficient process.

Although many Loctite products were developed for today's sophisticated manufacturing environment, the company still makes Krieble's original Loctite adhesive, sold in a familiar red bottle known around the world.

{O}FFERING 18TH-CENTURY CHARM COMBINED WITH 21ST-CENTURY amenities, Avon Old Farms Hotel/Classic Hotels of Connecticut defines elegance in the heart of the scenic Farmington River Valley. Founded by the Brighenti family as a 24-unit motel in 1955, the hotel has grown into a 160-room showplace of Connecticut style, sophistication, and luxury. ✲ From the moment guests enter

the hotel, they know their stays will be unique. Warmth radiates throughout a building finely appointed with brass chandeliers, curving staircases, and antique furniture. The decor also includes 400 original watercolors of Farmington Valley, painted by local artists.

The 160 guest rooms include fresh flowers, thick towels, and other personal touches. Guests receive a complimentary continental breakfast, a choice of newspapers, and use of an exercise room, sauna, and outdoor pool. In the luxury wing, guests are treated to romantic, poster beds and handmade desks and nightstands.

Beautiful grounds and superb dining greatly enrich the Avon Old Farms Hotel experience. With 20 meticulously landscaped acres, attractive meeting rooms, and a ballroom with enclosed terrace, the hotel hosts 70 weddings a year and other functions of up to 200 people. Seasons Restaurant and Pub presents American continental cuisine in an intimate

setting with a panoramic view of woodlands, wildlife, and a stream. On-site herb and vegetable gardens ensure fresh ingredients at Seasons for each and every meal.

Classic Hotels, Country Elegance

In 1996, Avon became one of the four family-owned and -operated hotels known as Classic Hotels of Connecticut. The Simsbury Inn offers 98 French-country-styled rooms and three top-rated dining facilities in Evergreens Restaurant, Nutmeg Café, and Twigs Lounge. The inn accommodates up to 300 people for meetings, corporate retreats, weddings, and banquets.

Guests of the 72-room Farmington Inn enjoy breakfast in the delightful Victoria's Café and have an easy stroll to area shops, museums, and historic homes. Country weddings and antiques are the order of the day at the Simsbury 1820 House, a lovely New England residence with 34 guest rooms. During the summer months, guests can enjoy their complimentary continental breakfast on the veranda.

Classic Hotels are in Farmington Valley, home of the Hill-Stead Museum, antique shops, and a variety of country activities including horse and crafts shows. Outdoor enthusiasts have skiing, golf, and hikes to the Heublein Tower atop Talcott Mountain, plus canoeing, tubing, and fishing. With Hartford just 15 minutes away, visitors also can visit the Mark Twain House, Wadsworth Atheneum, and other destinations.

For more than 40 years, Avon Old Farms Hotel has offered the finest in hospitality, dining, and atmosphere, providing travelers with a special place in the heart of Connecticut.

FOUNDED AS A 24-UNIT MOTEL IN 1955, AVON OLD FARMS HOTEL/ CLASSIC HOTELS OF CONNECTICUT HAS GROWN INTO A 160-ROOM SHOWPLACE OF CONNECTICUT STYLE, SOPHISTICATION, AND LUXURY (TOP).

BEAUTIFUL GROUNDS AND SUPERB DINING GREATLY ENRICH THE AVON OLD FARMS HOTEL EXPERIENCE (BOTTOM).

Rensselaer at Hartford

{ THE MESSAGE EMANATING FROM RENSSELAER POLYTECHNIC INSTITUTE (RPI), the nation's oldest private technological university, located in Troy, New York, is "Why not change the world?" It is a goal reminiscent of a time when United Aircraft Corporation (UAC)—now United Technologies—was searching for an esteemed educational institution that would bring graduate education to its Hartford workforce. }

WITH TECHNOLOGY EMERGING AS A COMPETITIVE ADVANTAGE IN VIRTUALLY EVERY INDUSTRY, RENSSELAER AT HARTFORD CONTINUES TO SERVE AS A LEADING EDUCATIONAL RESOURCE FOR HARTFORD'S TECHNOLOGICAL AND CORPORATE COMMUNITY.

TODAY, MORE THAN 2,000 STUDENTS PURSUE GRADUATE DEGREES AT RENSSELAER AT HARTFORD.

CHRISTOPHER NAVIN

CHRISTOPHER NAVIN

The brainchild of UAC Chairman of the Board H.M. Horner and UAC President W.P. Gwinn, RPI of Connecticut—later renamed The Hartford Graduate Center, and since 1997, Rensselaer at Hartford—was realized when RPI President Livingston Houston accepted their proposal. Launched in 1955 with 212 students enrolled, a graduate school division of RPI was born in Connecticut.

Today, more than 2,000 students pursue graduate degrees at Rensselaer at Hartford. The Computer and Information Sciences Department, the Engineering Department, and the Lally School of Management and Technology offer degree programs reflecting current technological trends and needs of the business community. The faculty meets the rigorous academic standards of RPI, contributing to the Graduate School of Engineering maintaining a high national ranking in *U.S. News & World Report*. Rensselaer's Lally School of Management and Technology is an accredited member of the American Assembly of Collegiate Schools of Business (AACSB), the International Association for Management Education.

For more than 40 years, the mission of the Connecticut campus has been to "meet the lifelong learning needs of the experienced professional." Students bring with

them diverse professional backgrounds and perspectives, that enhance the collective learning experience. The faculty's considerable experience in business, industry, government, and nonprofit organizations helps shape a dynamic learning environment set amid actual business practices. Affiliation with the Troy campus enables Rensselaer to nurture the ties between research and the more pragmatic business world.

Flexible Degree Programs

Rensselaer at Hartford accommodates students' scheduling needs by offering graduate classes in the evenings and on weekends. Specialized schedules like the 30-month weekend MBA allow working professionals to take most classes on Friday nights and Saturdays. Rensselaer at Hartford also offers graduate certificates in computer science and engineering.

Students demonstrating a high level of professional and academic achievement can earn a master's degree in management through the Executive Master's Program. This highly selective program stresses the integration of management and technology, and prepares executives for senior positions in their organizations.

Another ongoing need for most businesses is to provide staff and managers with the necessary training in the latest management techniques and technology changes.

Rensselaer Learning Institute, an entrepreneurial unit within Rensselaer at Hartford, attracts thousands annually to their non-degree short courses, seminars, and workshops. Topics include computer information technology, leadership and executive development, technical and professional seminars, and PC desktop courses.

Serving Hartford and Beyond

Situated on 16 landscaped acres in downtown Hartford, Rensselaer occupies its own eight-story building. The institution also has been educating professionals in southeastern Connecticut since 1977 at its southeastern Connecticut site.

Outside the Hartford campus, the staff and faculty have forged a bond with two neighborhood elementary schools, Barnard-Brown School and S.A.N.D. School. Many of the schools' students attend the Rensselaer Summer Computer Camp, an opportunity to reinforce computer technology—introduced in their classrooms—in a constructive and nurturing environment. The staff's volunteerism extends to Downtown Council programs and local shelters as well.

With technology emerging as a competitive advantage in virtually every industry, Rensselaer at Hartford continues to serve as a leading educational resource for Hartford's technological and corporate community.

T FIRST GLANCE, THE UNIVERSITY OF HARTFORD APPEARS TO BE an ordinary institution of higher learning. Its attractive, 320-acre main campus in suburban West Hartford offers classrooms, dormitories, libraries, a modern sports complex, and a performing arts center. ✻ A closer examination, however, reveals a setting that offers far more than a typical college education. In fact, the

University of Hartford
of Hartford

University of Hartford offers a variety of courses and programs that appeal to the entire community: lifelong education from the undergraduate level to continuing professional education; a variety of resources for area businesses, industries, governments, and non-profit organizations; and an array of rich cultural offerings.

Nine Schools in One

The school was chartered in 1957, when the Hartford Art School (founded by a group that included Mrs. Samuel Clemens), Hillyer College, and the Hartt School of Music were joined. Today, the university also includes schools of business; arts and sciences; education, nursing, and health professions; engineering; technology; and Hartford College for Women.

"The University of Hartford truly is one of a kind," says Walter Harrison, president. "Having varied schools facilitates individualized studies, such as the acoustics and music program that lets students combine a talent for engineering with a passion for music. It's the only program of its kind in the country. Other distinctive resources include both business and engineering applications centers where businesses, government agencies, and nonprofit organizations gain access to academic expertise while students obtain real-world experience."

Whether in the community or in the classroom, a student-faculty ratio of 13-to-1 fosters a supportive atmosphere. Faculty members are recognized experts, with 78 percent of them holding the top degree in their fields.

The university's 7,000 students come from nearly every state and 66 foreign countries. Among its notable alumni are International Paper CEO John Dillon; former astronaut Edgar Brisson; El Salvador President Francisco Flores; and professional athletic standouts Jeff Bagwell and Vin Baker.

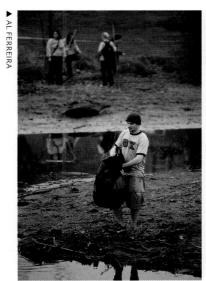

Fostering Community Service

The university is particularly proud of its Center for Community Service, which matches students, faculty, staff, and alumni with volunteer opportunities. "Service has become part of the university's culture," Harrison says. "Faculty look for ways to incorporate it into their curricula. For example, graphics design students have created flyers for local agencies. Students of criminal justice are analyzing data and helping residents of a Hartford neighborhood with crime prevention. The center is making a real difference in area communities and in the lives of our students and staff."

The school reaches out to area children as well. For example, the University of Hartford Magnet School, scheduled to open on the main campus in 2001, will serve 400 students in kindergarten through fifth grade from Hartford and five surrounding suburbs.

The university also enriches its environs with many cultural offer-

ings. Theater, opera, dance, music, exhibitions, and lectures are available year-round. At the music school, the Grammy-winning Emerson String Quartet has an exclusive teaching and performing residency. The Museum of American Political Life showcases the country's largest private collection of political memorabilia.

The University of Hartford's wealth of educational and cultural resources, strong business and government ties, and passion for community involvement form a solid foundation as it continues to make a difference in its community well into the future.

CLOCKWISE FROM TOP LEFT: THE UNIVERSITY OF HARTFORD ENCOURAGES ITS STUDENTS, FACULTY, AND STAFF TO TAKE AN ACTIVE ROLE IN COMMUNITY SERVICE.

A FUN RUN IN SPRING 1999 TO CELEBRATE THE INAUGURATION OF PRESIDENT WALTER HARRISON ATTRACTED PARTICIPANTS FROM THE UNIVERSITY OF HARTFORD AND EXTERNAL COMMUNITIES. THE SPORTS CENTER IN THE BACKGROUND IS HOME TO DIVISION ONE ATHLETICS, AND ITS HEALTH AND FITNESS CLUB MEMBERSHIP PROGRAM IS AVAILABLE TO AREA RESIDENTS.

SPEAKING FOR FAR FEWER THAN "60 MINUTES," CBS' AWARD-WINNING JOURNALIST MIKE WALLACE RECEIVED AN HONORARY DEGREE AT A RECENT UNIVERSITY OF HARTFORD COMMENCEMENT.

THE UNIVERSITY'S CLASSROOM SETTINGS ARE SMALL AND INTERACTIVE. A 13-TO-1 RATIO OF STUDENTS TO FACULTY FOSTERS AN ATMOSPHERE OF SUPPORTIVE LEARNING.

NOW IN ITS SECOND GENERATION OF DIRECT-FAMILY MANAGEMENT, Konover is one of the largest and most successful privately held commercial real estate companies on the East Coast. ✳ By steadily diversifying and expanding its services for more than 40 years, Konover has evolved into a full-service source for commercial real estate development, leasing, property management, acquisition,

construction, and general contracting. Konover has owned or developed more than 16.5 million square feet of retail, office, hotel, and specialty properties, and multifamily residential communities.

Together, Konover's two distinct companies—Konover & Associates, Inc. and Konover Investments Corporation—bring a world-class portfolio of real estate services to the East Coast.

Distinct Companies, Unique Specialties

Based in Farmington, Connecticut, Konover & Associates specializes in the development, leasing management, and construction of retail properties and community shopping centers. The company identifies and secures prime East Coast loca-

tions for national, regional, and local retail clients ranging from big-box retailers and supermarket chains to drugstores, restaurants, and theaters.

Today, Konover & Associates manages more than 70 shopping centers from Maine to Florida with a combined area of more than 8 million square feet. Konover & Associates has a tradition of retained ownership, having developed 80 percent of the centers in its current portfolio. Hartford-area projects include Simsbury Commons in Simsbury, Stop & Shop Plaza in Enfield, and Bishops Corner East and Bishops Corner West in West Hartford. In addition, the company's construction affiliate, Konover Construction Corporation (KCC), is one of the largest merit contractors in the state. KCC completed more than 2.4 million square feet of construction in 1999, and is ranked 206th among the nation's top 400 construction companies. KCC is also ranked 20th in the nation for retail interior fit-up, and ninth in the nation for shell construction of retail centers.

Konover Investments Corporation (KIC), headquartered in West Hartford, owns, develops, and manages office buildings, multifamily residential communities, hotels, and mixed-use and specialty properties such as structured parking, assisted

living, and exhibition facilities in the eastern United States. Like Konover & Associates, KIC manages properties owned by third parties as well as its own assets. Currently, KIC manages approximately 1 million square feet of office space, including One Century Tower, which the firm developed into New Haven's premier office tower. KIC also manages 4,500 apartment units, many of which are in the Hartford area, and more than 1,000 hotel rooms, including the Sheraton Bradley Hotel, the only on-site hotel at Bradley International Airport.

KIC's specialty property portfolio includes the Connecticut Expo Center in Hartford, one of the finest exhibition centers in the area, and Middlewoods, an assisted living facility in Farmington.

A History of Growth and Success

Konover was founded in 1959 by Simon Konover, a Holocaust survivor who immigrated to Hartford after World War II and began his career laying floor tile. As the suburbs grew, and with the advent of discount stores, Konover built his first hotel and shopping center. Over the years, he developed the company into one of the top real estate organizations in the United States. Still active in the business,

KONOVER INVESTMENTS CORPORATION MANAGES MORE THAN 1,000 HOTEL ROOMS, INCLUDING THE SHERATON BRADLEY HOTEL, THE ONLY ON-SITE HOTEL AT BRADLEY INTERNATIONAL AIRPORT.

AMONG THE MANY PROPERTIES OWNED, DEVELOPED, AND MANAGED BY KONOVER INVESTMENTS CORPORATION IS CENTURY TOWER IN NEW HAVEN, CONNECTICUT.

he is chairman emeritus of Konover & Associates and CEO of Konover Investments Corporation, while his son Michael is chairman and CEO of Konover & Associates, Inc.

The Konover companies have shared a commitment to excellence from the beginning. Putting customers first, they pride themselves on being fair and dependable in their business dealings while maintaining the highest ethical and quality standards. They deliver what they promise. As a result, they have built long-lasting relationships with clients, many of whom have invited the New England developer to become involved in their own expansions into new geographic markets throughout the Atlantic seaboard and into the Midwest.

Konover has withstood tumultuous economic cycles while other developers have come and gone. With an entrepreneurial spirit, the company succeeds by focusing on its core businesses while enhancing its operations, employing talented associates who are dedicated to customer service, expanding geographically at the request of clients, and investing in new technology.

A Legacy of Responsible Development

Konover has a proud history of responsible development that enhances local economies. The company credits its success to finding new ways of working with community and other groups to achieve common ground on which to build understanding and consensus, be a catalyst for progress, maximize the value of assets in its portfolio, and achieve positive results.

Konover & Associates developed the first full-service supermarket in Hartford's Upper Albany neighborhood in the 1970s and participated in the rebirth of the Berlin Turnpike as a shopping destination. In 1999, the company transformed an outdated mall into Simsbury Commons, a revitalized community center that includes a movie theater, restaurants, a large bookstore, and a police substation. In Keene, Konover & Associates, Inc. is working with local officials to preserve the integrity of ecologically sensitive wetlands while developing a new retail shopping center.

In Hartford, KIC has refurbished several older buildings, preserving their charm while bringing new business to the downtown area. The firm is pursuing development of an exciting property that would include a hotel, offices, restaurants, shopping, and parking, enriching and enlivening the capital city.

In addition to being a responsible developer, Konover tries to mix charity and corporate responsibility into everything it does. The firm has a proud history of giving back to the community.

The company actively supports charities and local programs in the communities in which its 800 associates live and work. These include the Hole in the Wall Gang Camp for children with cancer and serious blood diseases, the Food Allergy Center at Connecticut Children's Medical Center, the Juvenile Diabetes Foundation, and Jonathan's Dream Playground.

Konover will continue to prosper by focusing on the East Coast markets that have defined it as a leader, hiring top talent, and actively seeking and developing properties that fit its portfolio and offer the best potential for growth.

{1961-1989}

1961   UNIVERSITY OF CONNECTICUT HEALTH CENTER

1965   CONNECTICUT STATE UNIVERSITY SYSTEM

1967   UPDIKE, KELLY & SPELLACY, P.C.

1970   TAI SOO KIM PARTNERS, ARCHITECTS

1971   CROWNE PLAZA HARTFORD DOWNTOWN

1972   SIMIONE SCILLIA LARROW & DOWLING LLC

1974   HARTFORD ADVOCATE

1975   HARTFORD CIVIC CENTER VETERANS MEMORIAL
        COLISEUM AND EXHIBITION CENTER

1976   WINDSOR MARKETING GROUP

1979   ESPN, INC.

1979   EXECUTIVE GREETINGS, INC.

1980   MARTINO & BINZER

1980   ROME McGUIGAN SABANOSH, P.C.

1984   THE ALLIED GROUP INC.

1984   FARMSTEAD TELEPHONE GROUP, INC.

1984   TALLÁN, INC.

1987   FAMILYMEDS, INC.

University of Connecticut Health Center

THE UNIVERSITY OF CONNECTICUT HEALTH CENTER IS A VIBRANT organization that is a hub of medical and dental education, world-class biomedical research, and quality health care services for Connecticut citizens. The Health Center is home to the UConn School of Medicine, the UConn School of Dental Medicine, and a fast-growing research center, as well as the John Dempsey Hospital and many

outpatient services. Founded in 1961, the Health Center is based in Farmington, about 10 miles west of Hartford.

Educating Physicians and Dentists

The Health Center is the only academic medical center in the country where medical and dental schools were founded concurrently. At the Health Center, medical and dental students essentially share a common curriculum for the first two years of their four-year programs. Thus, UConn's dental students receive a particularly strong foundation in the biomedical sciences and are awarded the doctor of dental medicine (DMD) degree.

Today, the UConn School of Dental Medicine is among the top five such schools in the country, and a newly revamped curriculum at the UConn School of Medicine has received national acclaim.

Each year, about 320 students enroll in the MD program, and

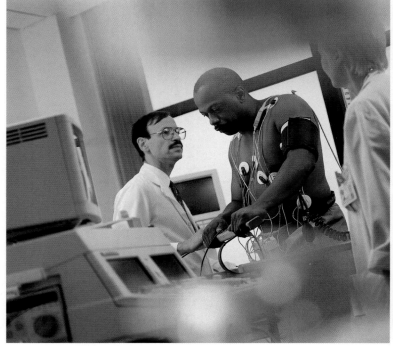

about 160 work toward the DMD. Admission to both schools is highly competitive, though preferential consideration is offered to qualified Connecticut residents.

In addition, more than 500 newly graduated physicians from throughout the United States come to the Hartford area every year for residency programs in internal medicine,

SENSITIVE AND SOPHISTICATED TECHNOLOGY ASSISTS CARDIOLOGISTS AT THE UNIVERSITY OF CONNECTICUT HEALTH CENTER'S JOHN DEMPSEY HOSPITAL IN FARMINGTON.

MEDICAL AND DENTAL STUDENTS ARE APPLAUDED BY THEIR PROFESSORS DURING COMMENCEMENT CEREMONIES EVERY SPRING AT THE UCONN HEALTH CENTER.

surgical specialties, primary care, and more. Training occurs at the Health Center and in community hospitals throughout Greater Hartford.

As a part of the University of Connecticut, the Health Center offers advanced study in the biomedical sciences. In addition to programs in medicine (MD) and dental medicine (DMD), programs offered also include doctoral degrees in biomedical science (PhD), as well as master's degrees in public health and dental science, postdoctoral fellowships, residency programs providing specialty training for new physicians and dentists, and continuing education for practicing health care professionals.

Remarkable Patient Care

During its recent review by the Joint Commission on Accreditation of Healthcare Organizations, the John Dempsey Hospital was awarded the commission's highest possible rating: accreditation with commendation. This distinction is earned by only 12 percent of American hospitals. At the same time, the state Office of Health Care Access ranked John Dempsey Hospital the most cost efficient of the state's 32 hospitals.

Due in great part to John Dempsey's distinguished research and teaching environment, the 204-bed facility offers programs including the region's only Bone Marrow Transplant Unit, high-tech cardiology services, and award-winning outpatient surgical care.

The John Dempsey Hospital is also noteworthy for its neonatal intensive care unit (NICU), the largest and oldest unit of its kind in the region. Supplementing its NICU services are the hospital's own transport vehicles, which are used to transport critically ill and premature infants from community hospitals all over the state to the Health Center.

Outpatient services at the Health Center include the only emergency department in the Farmington Valley, as well as an urgent care center. Other services include the UConn Cancer Center, orthopedics, rehabilitation and sports medicine services, geriatrics, hypertension services, dermatology, and more. Primary care physicians see patients at the Farmington campus, as well as at offices in Simsbury and Bloomfield.

The Health Center also reaches out to the community by presenting informative programs on disease prevention, clinical research, and new treatments. Information about health care and clinical services is available at the Health Center's clinic's Web site, www.uconnhealth.org.

World-Class Research

The UConn Health Center is committed to maintaining high-quality research programs. In 1999, the Health Center opened an 11-story Academic Research Building, which expanded its laboratory space by more than 40 percent. The new laboratory space has already helped the Health Center to recruit top researchers from across the nation and secure additional research funding.

Biomedical research at the Health Center today will help lead to tomorrow's cures in areas such as cancer, heart disease, and arthritis.

In addition, the Health Center is home to prestigious nationally funded research centers such as the Claude Pepper Older Americans Independence Center, Alcohol Research Center, and Connecticut Clinical Chemosensory Research Center.

Clinical research at the Health Center is facilitated by the Lowell Weicker General Clinical Research Center, and intellectual endeavors of all kinds are supported by the Lyman Maynard Stowe Library, which is the regional medical library for New England. The library is one of just eight in the National Network of Libraries of Medicine. The public benefits from this resource, with its free use and its many connections to local libraries.

Information about the University of Connecticut Health Center is featured at www.uchc.edu.

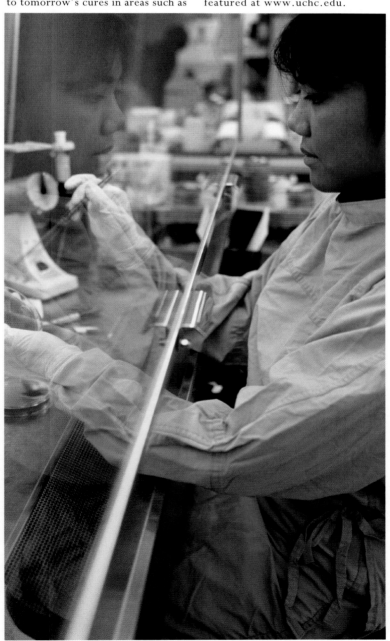

UConn Health Center scientists conduct groundbreaking biomedical research specializing in cancer, neurological function, and diseases of the bones and joints, such as osteoporosis, arthritis, and more.

ROM ITS ROOTS IN 19TH-CENTURY NORMAL SCHOOLS, THE CONNECTICUT State University System (CSU) has evolved into a technologically advanced university for the people, where a quality education is within reach of anyone with a desire to learn. CSU's universities—Central, Eastern, Southern, and Western—provide a comprehensive curriculum that ranges from liberal arts and sciences to business, education, nursing,

and social work. Approximately 34,000 students are enrolled in more than 130 academic programs leading to baccalaureate, graduate, and professional degrees, as well as career advancement. CSU's four schools, each initially established to train teachers, share one mission today—to encourage Connecticut students of all ages, races, religions, national origins, and social conditions to develop to their full potential.

Four Universities: Central, Eastern, Southern, Western

Established in 1849, Central Connecticut State University was the state's first public institution of higher education. Today, the New Britain campus offers studies in business, liberal arts, teacher education and professional studies, science, and other disciplines. Central's School of Technology is the state's largest public, four-year school of technology, with a curriculum that balances theory and practicality. The university encourages a global perspective with foreign language study, an international faculty and visiting scholars from abroad, and a Center of Excellence that coordinates student exchanges in the United States, Europe, Asia, and South America. CSU's largest school,

with nearly 12,000 graduate and undergraduate students, Central has an impressive computerized library with more than 500,000 volumes.

CSU's second-oldest university, Eastern Connecticut State University, opened in 1889. Today, it offers an outstanding liberal arts and science curriculum, and, as CSU's smallest school, cares for its nearly 5,000 full- and part-time undergraduates as individuals in the tradition of a small liberal arts college. Students from more than 30 countries around the globe enrich campus life in Willimantic and enliven the intellectual environment. Eastern's students can supplement their classroom studies with valuable internships

and field experience, working with faculty in an on-campus greenhouse, planetarium, TV and radio station, art gallery, or theater. Wickware Planetarium is an educational resource for Connecticut residents of all ages.

Since 1893, Southern Connecticut State University students have embraced their New Haven location. Nursing students gain unparalleled experience at Yale-New Haven Hospital, while computer science majors find inspiration in Science Park. Southern's innovative programs include the School of Communication, Information, and Library Science, blending traditional and modern disciplines of communication such as library science, computer

DAVIDSON HALL, LOCATED AT CENTRAL CONNECTICUT STATE UNIVERSITY, WAS ONE OF THE FIRST CAMPUS FACILITIES FOR WHAT IS TODAY THE CONNECTICUT STATE UNIVERSITY SYSTEM (CSU) (RIGHT).

FOR APPROXIMATELY 34,000 STUDENTS, CSU'S UNIVERSITIES PROVIDE A COMPREHENSIVE CURRICULUM RANGING FROM LIBERAL ARTS AND SCIENCES TO BUSINESS, EDUCATION, NURSING, AND SOCIAL WORK (LEFT).

science, journalism, and communications. The Center for the Environment offers interdisciplinary studies for science students and future teachers. Southern has more than 7,000 full-time undergraduates and, with almost 4,000 graduate students, is CSU's premier institution for advanced study.

Western Connecticut State University was founded in 1903, and serves 5,700 graduate and undergraduate students on two campuses. Undergraduates at the Weather Center in Danbury forecast conditions for towns, utilities, businesses, and the media. Besides offering the state's only meteorology degree, Western is known for its performing arts, business, justice, and environmental studies programs. Future managers and entrepreneurs in the Ancell School of Business have close relationships with local business people, while students planning careers in corrections and law enforcement or preparing for law school attend the Division of Justice and Law Administration. Western also offers unique opportunities through the Jane Goodall Center for Excellence in Environmental Studies.

Enhanced Educational Opportunities

In 1998, the State of Connecticut invested $21 million in a state-of-the-art telecommunications infrastructure to connect its universities to the world and to foster lifelong learning. On every campus throughout the state, smart classrooms enhance teaching and extend courses to students in the CSU system, as well as to public schools, libraries, and businesses. CSU is upgrading its own libraries with full-text electronic data sources, and is supplementing existing electronic catalogs to open a world of resources. Ultimately, every classroom at each campus will be linked to the Internet and CSU's voice and data network.

CSU has also added an exciting dimension for learning without regard to time, location, or circumstance: OnlineCSU, at www.onlinecsu. ctstateu.edu. The system features dozens of full-credit courses and a complete degree program—the Master of Library Science—plus course registration, advisers, and support for technical and content questions. OnlineCSU is providing new learning opportunities for

students around the globe. Ten courses kicked off the venture in the fall of 1998, with 43 offered in the spring semester in 2000. Hundreds of courses have gone online since the system's start-up. Students from all over the United States and the world have expressed interest in OnlineCSU.

CSU Chancellor William Cibes Jr. says OnlineCSU works because, unlike many other distance learning programs, faculty are the heart of the system—designing, teaching, and owning the courses' intellectual content. "It is a wonderful example of CSU's synergy, allowing us to com-

bine the strengths of our four universities to offer new and convenient learning opportunities," Cibes says. Over time, OnlineCSU will include additional degree programs, certificate programs, conferences, and executive leadership academies.

The university will continue to explore the ways that technology can help learners access the education they need to compete in today's world. CSU will continue putting a high-quality education—whether accessed through the latest technology or through the traditional classroom environment—within the reach of all Connecticut citizens.

CSU WILL CONTINUE PUTTING A HIGH-QUALITY EDUCATION— WHETHER ACCESSED THROUGH THE LATEST TECHNOLOGY OR THROUGH THE TRADITIONAL CLASSROOM ENVIRONMENT—WITHIN THE REACH OF ALL CONNECTICUT CITIZENS (TOP).

THE CLOCK TOWER AND J. EUGENE SMITH LIBRARY ARE NOTABLE LANDMARKS OF EASTERN CONNECTICUT STATE UNIVERSITY (BOTTOM).

Updike, Kelly & Spellacy, P.C.

A team of talented attorneys, combined with a far-ranging practice and a flexible organization, enables Updike, Kelly & Spellacy, P.C. (UKS) to offer clients a potent combination: the resources, range, and depth of a large law firm, plus the hands-on involvement of a small practice. For more than 30 years, UKS has been helping its clients anticipate and manage risk, and find

pragmatic solutions to problems. With 70 attorneys, the firm has its main office in downtown Hartford, with smaller offices in New Haven and Stamford—a network that enables UKS to serve clients throughout Connecticut.

The firm has more than 20 areas of practice that span a wide range of specialties, including litigation, municipal, corporate, and environmental law, and commercial lending and banking. Through its UKS Public Affairs Corporation, the firm has an active government relations practice through which it maintains effective relationships with municipal, state, and national leaders across the political spectrum, offering another means of serving clients.

Talent, Tenacity, and Flexibility

The attorneys at UKS enjoy an energetic, collegial atmosphere, and relish working together as a team. They strive diligently to respond to the needs of their clients, to understand the business environment, and to anticipate developments in a dynamic discipline. UKS attorneys are known for their aggressive style, eloquence in the courtroom, and tenacity at the negotiating table. A

saying at the firm is "it is our goal to move mountains for our clients—or, when preferable, to navigate around them on our clients' behalf."

The firm's entrepreneurial culture and structure give it the flexibility to marshal appropriate resources for each situation and to obtain results efficiently. The area of major real estate development provides two recent examples of the benefits that clients derive from this approach. The developer of Buckland Hills in Manchester—at more than 100 acres, one of the state's largest regional malls—benefited from both the firm's organization and its breadth of knowledge. While another practice might have assigned the work to its real estate department exclusively, UKS assembled a team with expertise in environmental law, government relations, public finance, and commercial litigation, as well as real estate.

Elsewhere, developers of another major regional mall, Brass Mill Center in Connecticut's Naugatuck Valley, discovered that UKS attorneys frequently exceed expectations. The firm not only identified a site, but also secured a $45 million federal, state, and local funding package to address environmental issues, all of which were resolved.

Additional client benefits come from the firm's participation in Commercial Law Affiliates, a prestigious network of 5,000 attorneys in 70 countries. The only member firm in Connecticut, UKS was selected in 1991 for its expertise and reputation, and is monitored by the organization to ensure continued quality. Through this coveted affiliation, UKS furnishes clients with information, professional advice, and legal representation throughout the United States and around the world.

Community Involvement

UKS attorneys are community leaders, most particularly in the national, state, and local political milieus. Cofounder Peter Kelly, for example, is a past treasurer of the Democratic National Committee and former chairman of the MetroHartford Chamber of Commerce. The firm includes a former mayor of East Hartford, Republican and Democratic town party chairmen, and members of municipal boards and commissions.

Updike, Kelly & Spellacy is committed to the strongest possible advocacy on behalf of its clients, and to bringing its significant personal and professional resources to the table and working as a winning team.

BOURKE G. SPELLACY (LEFT) AND PETER G. KELLY ARE COFOUNDERS OF UPDIKE, KELLY & SPELLACY, P.C. (UKS).

TEAMS OF UKS ATTORNEYS WORK TO RESPOND TO CLIENT NEEDS (TOP RIGHT AND BELOW).

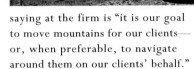

T ai Soo Kim Partners, Architects has amassed a portfolio of work spanning three continents—from North America to North Africa to Asia. Tai Soo Kim, who studied architecture in his native Korea and at Yale University, founded the firm in 1970, calling it the Hartford Design Group. He has subsequently created a partnership with two talented architects: Ryszard Szczypek, who earned the

American Institute of Architects (AIA) Student Medal at Syracuse University and joined Kim in 1974, and T. Whitcomb Iglehart, a Yale architecture graduate who joined the firm in 1985.

At first, the Hartford firm earned recognition for its civic architecture in a range of building types, from senior centers and schools to a submarine training facility. In the 1980s, the firm advanced its profile with institutional projects such as the Gray Cultural Center for the University of Hartford and the 300,000-square-foot National Museum of Contemporary Art in Seoul. In the 1990s, the firm won even larger commissions, including

a 4 million-square-foot retail and entertainment center in Seoul's Central City, and the master plan for Hartford's Learning Corridor, an urban, K-12 educational campus occupying a full city block near Trinity College. In 1999, the U.S. Department of State commissioned the firm to design a new embassy in Tunisia.

Honored for Design Excellence

Since its founding, the firm has received many design awards, including the AIA Medal of Honor for the Middlebury Elementary School, deemed "a marvelously refreshing learning environment"; the Korean National Department

of Construction & Transportation Grand Prize for the LG research and development park; and an AIA Honor Award for Interiors for the Helen and Harry Gray Court in Hartford's Wadsworth Atheneum.

With nearly 30 people on staff, Tai Soo Kim Partners is small enough for the partners to remain integrally involved in design work. A small office in Seoul facilitates the overseas work. Whether a school, a museum, or corporate headquarters, the firm's work is recognized for its elegance, its simplicity, and its harmony with cultural or built environments as well as its fresh perspective.

Clockwise from right: Whether designing the Helen & Harry Gray Court Wadsworth Atheneum; the Gray Cultural Center at the University of Hartford; or the Connecticut Education Association's Capitol Place, Tai Soo Kim Partners, Architects lifts the human spirit with a fresh perspective.

▲ TAI SOO KIM

▲ NICK WHEELER

▲ ROBERT BENSON

Crowne Plaza Hartford Downtown

{ FROM TOP TO BOTTOM, THE CROWNE PLAZA HARTFORD DOWNTOWN is the smart choice for travelers who want outstanding accommodations, superior guest services, and a central location when visiting Hartford for business or pleasure. From the upper floors, guests can enjoy panoramic views of the capital city, as well as the beautiful Connecticut River and distant green hills, while in the attractive lobby, the doormen }

and desk clerks welcome visitors with sincere smiles.

Situated between Main and Morgan streets since 1971, the Crowne Plaza is convenient to the city's major businesses and destinations, such as the Hartford Stage Company, Wadsworth Atheneum, Mark Twain House, Trinity College, University of Hartford, Travelers, Fleet, and Cigna.

An investment of nearly $14 million in interior and exterior renovations in 1998 led to the hotel's rebranding. Now known as the Crowne Plaza Hartford Downtown, the hotel provides guests with top-of-the-line luxury.

FROM THE CROWNE PLAZA HARTFORD DOWNTOWN'S UPPER FLOORS, GUESTS CAN ENJOY PANORAMIC VIEWS OF THE CAPITAL CITY, AS WELL AS THE BEAUTIFUL CONNECTICUT RIVER AND DISTANT GREEN HILLS, WHILE IN THE ATTRACTIVE LOBBY, THE DOORMEN AND DESK CLERKS WELCOME VISITORS WITH SINCERE SMILES.

Caring for Savvy Travelers

The 18-story hotel, the new address for the savvy traveler™, features 350 handsomely appointed guest rooms, including five suites. The oversized rooms are furnished with coffeemakers, irons and full-sized ironing boards, hair dryers, and makeup/shaving mirrors. For the business traveler, the guest room also functions as a virtual office on the road, with Internet access with dataport and a comfortable, ergonomically designed desk and chair.

The Crowne Plaza Club executive floor is an amenity extended to guests with special key access. The central hospitality room serves a complimentary continental breakfast Monday through Friday, as well as evening hors d'oeuvres and beverages. All guests have use of an underground garage, an exercise room, an outdoor swimming pool, and a sundeck. Breakfast, lunch, and a dinner menu are available in the comfortable Bristol Bar & Grill off the main lobby.

Besides providing guests with superior services, Crowne Plaza can also accommodate meetings and banquets of up to 500 guests.

The hotel has more than 7,000 square feet of event space, including 13 rooms that can easily be reconfigured for conferences, corporate seminars, wedding receptions, reunions, banquets, and other special events. A professional event coordinator assists planners with every detail to ensure success, from menu selections, decorations, and entertainment to audiovisual support and other services.

Crowne Plaza Hartford Downtown employees take pride in offering guests a thoroughly pleasant experience, not merely a place to stay. Every employee is trained in the four principles that form the company's core philosophy: incredibly friendly employees, spotlessly clean and well-maintained hotels, exceeding expectations at every opportunity, and doing the right thing. Office spaces without walls or doors emphasize the company's commitment to communication and teamwork.

Large enough to provide superior accommodations and services for guests, but small enough to offer friendly, personal attention and the flexibility to meet a variety of needs, Crown Plaza Hartford Downtown plans to continue to be the hotel of choice for the savvy traveler.

SITUATED BETWEEN MAIN AND MORGAN STREETS SINCE 1971, THE CROWNE PLAZA IS CONVENIENT TO MAJOR BUSINESSES AND DESTINATIONS IN THE CITY.

THROUGH DEDICATION TO CLIENT NEEDS, AN ATTENTION TO SUPERIOR service, and the accessibility of its principals, Simione Scillia Larrow & Dowling LLC (SSLD) has become one of the top accounting firms in Connecticut, one that turns tactical accounting support into an enduring financial partnership. Clients' relationships with SSLD are based on mutual trust and shared success. With nearly three decades of experience,

the firm is committed to helping company owners, individuals, and families reach objectives that had seemed out of reach.

Founded in 1972 with offices in New Haven and Hartford, SSLD offers financial reporting and auditing services. Management consulting and tax services are provided through Simione Scillia Larrow & Dowling Advisors LLC (Advisors), a Centerprise company. Management consulting services include accounting and administrative systems consulting, bankruptcy support, business consulting, computer systems consulting, financial services, fraud and investigative services, litigation advisory, and merger and acquisition services. Advisors offers tax services such as corporate tax, estate and gift tax planning, individual tax, sales and use tax, and tax representation.

With a staff of approximately 60 in Advisors and some 20 in SSLD, each firm provides professional services that grow with its clients. Both companies are large in terms of resources, but small when it comes to the personal attention their clients receive. A special synergy among the principals, staff, and clients ensures effective planning and cost-effective account management.

Four Client Specialties

Four areas of expertise—construction, government, manufacturing, and health care—form the core of SSLD's business. Having worked with clients within the construction business for 25 years, the firm is familiar with the financial dynamics that drive the industry. The firm understands the unique perspectives of general construction companies, insulation specialists, drywall companies, and even underwater construction companies. Specialized services unique to Advisors include claim consulting, surety credit, and bank financing consulting.

SSLD also knows the complex issues affecting government, whether state, municipal, or quasi-public entities. SSLD has complemented its core auditing capabilities with services that help clients achieve and maintain excellent standards of financial accountability and performance. Among its services are audits and financial reporting, OMB Circular A-133, and single audit.

Manufacturing and distribution firms also benefit from SSLD's impressive professional services as well as its experience. Advisors provides management information systems (MIS) effectiveness reviews and soft-

ware evaluations, and offers distribution channel analysis, facilities planning, and more. In addition, actuarial, benefits, and compensation planning services are offered.

Both SSLD and Advisors have considerable experience in helping health care providers and consultants face the present and prepare for the future. Each firm's expertise includes long-term care services, home health care services, physicians and other health care professionals, and health care organizations.

Simione Scillia Larrow & Dowling's clients include large and small companies alike. Regardless of the clients' size or need, the firm is dedicated to providing accounting services that are second to none.

CONSTRUCTION, GOVERNMENT, MANUFACTURING, AND HEALTH CARE FORM THE CORE BUSINESS OF SIMIONE SCILLIA LARROW & DOWLING LLC.

Hartford Advocate

I N 1974, THE UNITED STATES WAS LESS THAN A YEAR OUT OF THE VIETNAM War, and a scandal called Watergate was undoing President Richard Nixon. Many Americans were eager for social change. The timing was right for an alternative voice in the media, one that would write the stories the mainstream press wouldn't cover or those that were underreported. ✸ That September, the *Hartford Advocate*—distributed initially as the

ValleyAdvocate—entered the market on a mission to effect positive social change and give a voice to those who had none. While at first it caught the Insurance City's eye for its hip personality, the newspaper soon developed a following for investigative news coverage and its support of the local arts scene.

Questioning the Status Quo

Today, the *Advocate* is one of the oldest of some 140 alternative newspapers in the country, and remains dedicated to questioning the status quo. The paper's philosophy has not changed with new ownership. In April 1999, the *Hartford Courant* bought New Mass Media, Inc., a chain of alternative weeklies that include the *Hartford Advocate*. The sale to an establishment newspaper only strengthened the *Advocate*'s resolve. The paper celebrated its 25th-year anniversary two months early, making a symbolic statement just before Independence Day. In an editorial, Editor Janet Reynolds quoted Fyodor Dostoyevsky: "What man wants is simple, independent choice, whatever that independence may cost and wherever it may lead."

For its part, the *Courant* has respected the *Advocate*'s value and has not tried to influence its coverage.

Reynolds speaks fervently about the role of alternative weeklies in today's world. "Many cities have just one daily newspaper, and with no competition, they lose their edge," she says. "Meanwhile, sound bites have replaced thought-provoking, in-depth coverage. A healthy democracy demands an alternative media."

The paper's work has admirers, even among those it takes to task. In 1999, the state of Connecticut's judicial branch, which includes lawyers and justices, honored the *Advocate* Justice Project series with a First Amendment Award for Excellence in Judicial Reporting. The series exposed problems within the state prison guard system, looked at judges and prosecutors who abuse their powers, and examined troubles within a suburban police department.

Organizations like the New England Press Association, Society of Professional Journalists, and Association of Alternative Newspapers have also recognized the *Advocate*, citing the paper's design, reporting, and overall excellence.

Supporting Local Artists

Besides covering hard news, the *Advocate* boosts local artists with club listings and reviews. The newspaper is a catalog of local happenings—from music, art, and the stage to seminars, support services, and volunteerism.

Civic activism takes many forms. In 1984, the *Advocate* created the Best of the Bands, now called Grand Band Slam, to highlight the city's growing musical culture. Annually, readers and judges select the top local performers in categories ranging from gospel to hip-hop. The event also includes a free street festival that attracts thousands of fans.

In 1989, the *Advocate* and Hartford's Downtown Council co-founded the city's First Night, a family-centered New Year's Eve celebration. Another tradition is the Best Of poll, in which readers vote for their favorites in 200 categories—from dentists to beer to TV stations.

While promoting local culture, the *Hartford Advocate*'s overriding purpose is to protect its independence, continue to address injustices, and remain an alternative voice for Hartford, as it has for more than a quarter century.

OR MORE THAN 25 YEARS, THE HARTFORD CIVIC CENTER VETERANS
Memorial Coliseum and Exhibition Center has enlivened and entertained Connecticut's capital city. On average, more than 1.5 million
people a year pass through the turnstiles of the state's premier sports
and entertainment center to see an impressive array of world-class
sporting events, family shows, ice skating spectaculars, concerts,
trade shows, and special events.

The Civic Center has presented more than 550 concerts by 250 performers ranging from the Rolling Stones, to Billy Joel, Bruce Springsteen, Shania Twain, and Andrea Bocelli. Besides concerts, the Civic Center offers a wide range of programs, from the World Wrestling Federation (WWF) and Ringling Bros. and Barnum & Bailey Circus, to Champions on Ice and the Harlem Globetrotters. The University of Connecticut's men's and women's basketball teams call the Civic Center their home away from home, and consistently play before sellout crowds.

A Helping Hand from Madison Square Garden

As the facility's manager, New York's Madison Square Garden uses its extensive experience and industry relationships to ensure the quantity and quality of events in Hartford's attractive arena.

Soon after it assumed management responsibilities in 1997, the Garden, in conjunction with the Connecticut Development Authority, implemented and supervised a multimillion-dollar, two-year capital improvement program to enhance guests' overall experience. Phases of the renovation included the replacement of 16,500 seats, addition of a state-of-the-art sound system and the latest in video-operated lighting systems, renovation of team locker rooms, and upgrade of meeting rooms and the air-conditioning system.

Madison Square Garden also gave Hartford two professional sports teams—the Hartford Wolf Pack, the American Hockey League affiliate of the New York Rangers, and the New England Sea Wolves arena football team—which the Garden owns and operates.

Suites and clubs offer the most luxurious accommodations at the Civic Center. There are 45 executive suites, each furnished with

JERRY MARGOLIS

television monitors, cable television, and 10 to 12 plush seats. The Coliseum Club Restaurant can serve 150 people and, after dinner, its 310 tiered, luxury seats provide a superb view of the action on the floor. Another deluxe option, the Directors' Suite, has four televisions, a full-service bar, living-room-style seating, and exclusive use of 26 theater-style seats.

Exhibition Center Draws Visitors to Trade Shows

On the same level as the coliseum floor, a 68,000-square-foot Exhibition Center brings more than 250,000 people to Downtown Hartford each year for an average of 100 consumer and trade shows. Popular events include the Connect-

icut Marine Trade Association's Boat and Fishing Shows, Home Show, Bridal Expo, Christmas Craft Expo, and college and job fairs. The area's flexible facilities include two exhibition halls, an assembly hall, and nine meeting rooms that can accommodate from 12 to 1,200 people.

In cyberspace, the Civic Center's home at www.hartfordciviccenter. com is as technologically advanced as the building itself. The interactive site features 360-degree virtual tours of executive skyboxes, the Directors' Suite and Coliseum Club, entrances, exhibition spaces, and other special areas. The site also has an event calendar, enabling patrons to buy tickets on-line; handy seating charts; team links; and booking information.

From the plush executive seats in the coliseum to the spacious exhibition facilities on the lower level, the Hartford Civic Center's amenities ensure that guests will have an enjoyable visit. Its staff works hard to keep them returning to the facility, and expects that they will—for many generations to come.

SUITES AND CLUBS OFFER THE MOST LUXURIOUS ACCOMMODATIONS AT THE HARTFORD CIVIC CENTER VETERANS MEMORIAL COLISEUM AND EXHIBITION CENTER FOR AN IMPRESSIVE VIEW OF WORLD-CLASS SPORTING EVENTS, FAMILY SHOWS, ICE SKATING SPECTACULARS, CONCERTS, TRADE SHOWS, AND SPECIAL EVENTS (TOP).

ON AVERAGE, MORE THAN 1.5 MILLION PEOPLE A YEAR PASS THROUGH THE TURNSTILES OF THE CIVIC CENTER, THE STATE'S PREMIER SPORTS AND ENTERTAINMENT CENTER (BOTTOM).

JERRY MARGOLIS

Windsor Marketing Group

GENERATIONS AGO, NEIGHBORHOOD GROCERS LED SHOPPERS AROUND the store, pointing out specials. Today, busy shoppers dash into large supermarkets with only a vague idea of what they might buy. Windsor Marketing Group (WMG), a leading national producer of in-store signage and marketing programs, makes shopping easier. Its Path of Purchase℠ signs lead shoppers to advertised specials, promotions, and

holiday ideas, and from department to department, making the shopping experience easier and more affordable.

WMG's informative and educational signs benefit both consumers and store owners. They help shoppers navigate the store, find products, discover what's on sale, learn what services the store offers, and get recipes, cooking tips, and menu ideas.

The signs also encourage shoppers to buy on impulse and purchase larger quantities of shopping list items. For supermarket chains and independent store owners, signs are a cost-effective way to increase sales and profits.

WMG was the brainchild of Kevin Armata, now company CEO. Growing up in the business in his father's grocery store, Armata became interested in customers' buying habits. Later, as a salesman for a distributor of marking pens, his interest in supermarkets and market-

AT WINDSOR MARKETING GROUP'S (WMG) 20TH-ANNIVERSARY CELEBRATION, BEETLEMANIA FEATURED THE MUSIC AND CEO KEVIN ARMATA HOSTED THE FUN-FILLED EVENT.

COLORFUL PICTURE SIGNS™, A SPECIALTY OF WMG, ENLIVEN STORES AND COMMUNICATE WITH SHOPPERS.

ing continued. As Armata sold markers to food retailers to make hand-lettered signs, he realized the signs could be improved with sophisticated printing techniques, and founded Windsor Marketing Group in 1976.

A National Leader in In-Store Communication

WMG—which now assists more than 3,500 retailers, manufacturers, and distributors nationwide, including most national chains—has seen double-digit growth every year. The company is one of the nation's largest producers of signage, point-of-purchase, and in-store marketing communications programs, and is well on its way to becoming the leader in the in-store communications industry for retailers. WMG also works with toy store and drugstore retailers, automotive outlets, and home stores, to name just a few.

WMG offers all of the services needed for effective in-store communication, from initial consultation through post-installation evaluation. The process begins with an audit. A WMG marketing expert walks through a store, determines its Ease of Shopping Index℠, and proposes a customized solution based on the items requiring signage, program components such as weekly specials, item and price information, and other factors. The company ensures that in-store images and messages are consistent with circulars and other marketing materials.

The next step is the design and printing of high-quality signs for windows, aisles, counters, shelves, and special displays. WMG handles production at its 200,000-square-foot, state-of-the-art headquarters in Windsor Locks, Connecticut, where its proximity to Bradley International Airport allows for quick turnaround and smooth distribution to national accounts.

As a full-service company, WMG assists with installation. The firm can provide store personnel with instructional manuals and videos, or, if the client prefers, WMG will offer on-site support. Once signs are in place, WMG will analyze their effectiveness and recommend changes as appropriate.

In 2000, WMG introduced Picture Signs™, an affordable, colorful means to enliven stores and communicate prices and items. The signs are particularly effective in multilingual neighborhoods or in ethnic market areas.

Much of WMG's success lies in its entrepreneurial spirit, which encourages the company's staff to work collaboratively. Each year, Armata presents an enterprising employee with the prized Golden Maverick Award.

Entering its third decade, Windsor Marketing Group plans to invest in education and technology, as well as improve its customization techniques, to ensure that the company remains an industry leader in making stores easier to shop.

FROM ITS MODEST BEGINNING ON SEPTEMBER 7, 1979, AS THE FIRST 24-hour sports television network, ESPN has become one of the most recognized brands in the world and features the broadest multimedia platform in sports—including television, radio, the Internet, a magazine, books, and more. In two decades, the company has grown from one building on less than an acre to a campus of buildings on 43 acres.

The firm's growth has been so explosive that the *New York Times* selected ESPN as one of the brands to watch in the 21st century.

ESPN, Inc. features more than 40 businesses, most of which emanate from the company's world headquarters in Bristol, Connecticut. There are six domestic networks, including ESPN2, the fastest-growing cable network ever; ESPN Classic, which showcases the greatest stars and moments in sports with a current perspective; and ESPNEWS, an all-sports news channel. ESPN also operates digital pay networks, 19 international television networks, and syndication reaching 140 countries and territories in nine languages. ESPN Radio—the largest sports radio network in the world—has more than 600 affiliates and more than 100 full-time stations, including one in Hartford.

Outside of television and radio, the company offers ESPN.com, the leading sports content provider on the Internet; *ESPN The Magazine*, a biweekly publication with more than 1 million subscribers; and ESPN Zone, a group of dining and entertainment establishments.

ESPN attributes its remarkable brand success to this underlying distinction: it does not consider itself a company, but a major fan who is always passionate about sports. The company emphasizes teamwork, and continually focuses on delivering the best and most innovative sports programming and products with flair and humor, as shown by its promotions and on-air personalities. "This Is Sports Center"—an award-winning advertising campaign that *TV Guide* called one of the best in television history—is a perfect example of ESPN's distinctive style. These promotions, filmed in Bristol, have raised the profile not only of the network's flagship news program, but of ESPN's hometown as well.

Sharing Passions for Sports

Through these qualities—being passionate about sports and having fun—ESPN has established a bond with its audience, whom the organization calls fans, not viewers. In 1994, *Newsweek* columnist George Will captured the special loyalty of ESPN's fans: "If someone surreptitiously took everything but ESPN from my cable television package, it might be months before I noticed."

Beyond its business of sports, ESPN contributes to numerous local and national charities, while its employees and commentators participate in community outreach programs. The company has also committed to an ESPN-branded facility in the Adriaen's Landing development project in downtown Hartford and is exploring a branded presence in Bristol.

ESPN also enjoys unique and mutually beneficial relationships with Bristol and the state of Connecticut. The company is Bristol's largest taxpayer and employer, and its community roots will grow deeper with the planned addition of several major buildings, including a digital television center that will position ESPN and its fans for the next wave of technology and entertainment in sports.

ESPN is 80 percent owned by ABC, Inc., an indirect subsidiary of the Walt Disney Company. The Hearst Corporation holds a 20 percent interest in ESPN.

CLOCKWISE FROM TOP:
WITH AN EMPHASIS ON TEAMWORK AND A FOCUS ON DELIVERING THE BEST AND MOST INNOVATIVE SPORTS PROGRAMMING WITH FLAIR AND HUMOR, ESPN'S PRODUCTION PERSONNEL ARE HARD AT WORK IN THE SCREENING ROOM.

ANCHORS CHRIS BERMAN (LEFT) AND BOB LEY HOSTED ESPN'S 20TH ANNIVERSARY SHOW ON THE NETWORK'S FRONT YARD AT ESPN PLAZA.

ESPN IS BRISTOL'S LARGEST TAX-PAYER AND EMPLOYER, AND ITS COMMUNITY ROOTS WILL GROW DEEPER WITH THE PLANNED ADDITION OF SEVERAL MAJOR BUILDINGS, INCLUDING A DIGITAL TELEVISION CENTER THAT WILL POSITION THE NETWORK FOR THE NEXT WAVE OF TECHNOLOGY AND ENTERTAINMENT IN SPORTS.

Executive Greetings, Inc.

WHEN BUSINESSES THROUGHOUT THE UNITED STATES AND Canada want to project a professional image at an affordable price, they turn to Executive Greetings, Inc. (EGI), founded in 1979 and the nation's second-largest direct marketer in the imprinted business products industry. Today, EGI has 450 employees and hires 300 more for October through

December. The firm includes a 150,000-square-foot headquarters in New Hartford, a call center in New Britain, and a manufacturing facility in Grand Prairie, Texas. The company's 21 catalogs offer more than 18,000 items, including imprinted greeting cards, desk diaries, promotional items, forms, and stationery.

More than 80 percent of EGI's sales are personalized with customer names, logos, and custom messages. The firm's enormous selection ranges from pens, mugs, and key tags to appointment reminders for dental practices to T-shirts, golf balls, clocks, and executive bags. If a business needs any kind of imprinted item, EGI is likely to have it in several designs.

Nationally, EGI is the leader in seasonal and everyday greeting cards—a major part of its imprinting business. The company's versatile artists, who design all of its printed products, turn out more than 300 original designs every year.

EGI's popular catalogs, some of which date back to the early 1950s and 1960s, include *The Drawing Board*, *Grayarc*, *Brookhollow*, *Baldwin Cooke*, *Dental Ideabook*, and *U.S. Diary*. The firm's reputation for high quality, innovation, and excellent service has fostered customer loyalty.

During the past two decades, EGI has expanded its product lines by acquiring varied catalogs. In 1997, EGI bought *HRdirect*, adding personnel forms, labor law postings, employee service awards, and motivational posters. The addition of the *SA-SO* catalog in 1999 added safety and signage products, including parking signs, back braces, fire extinguishers, building and grounds products, and security items.

Sophisticated Marketing, Strong Customer Service

EGI's sophisticated marketing programs and information technology, along with its proprietary, three-year customer list of 950,000 names—one of the largest customer

lists in the industry—makes it possible to effectively reach existing and prospective customers. The company supplements catalog mailings with a major telemarketing effort and individual mailings tailored to targeted markets. In 1999, EGI sent out 72 million catalogs and individual mailings, which resulted in 550,000 orders. In the coming years, the company expects to fill more than 600,000 orders.

Superior service is at the heart of EGI, which has developed an automated fulfillment process that can handle a large volume of small orders. The company prints and ships customized orders in three to five days, and mails many non-imprinted items the day they are ordered. All customers receive professional service—whether they order by telephone, mail, fax, or

the Internet—and, because of EGI's substantial size, they enjoy affordable pricing. More than 80 percent of customers are repeat business, a rate that is among the highest in the industry.

EGI donates imprinted coffee mugs to the local senior center, a soup kitchen, and women's shelters, and gives pens and pencils to schools. The company also supports the town library, Little League, police department, Special Olympics, United Way, Lions Club, and many others. Lee Bracken, president of EGI, says, "We're proud of our employees, some of whom have been with us from the beginning. And, as one of the largest employers in northeastern Connecticut, we enjoy giving back to our community." Entering its third decade, EGI remains a leader in the community and a national leader in the business-to-business direct marketing industry.

Farmstead Telephone Group, Inc.

{E}AST HARTFORD IS THE HOME OF FARMSTEAD TELEPHONE GROUP, Inc., the nation's largest supplier of both refurbished and new Avaya Communication telephone parts, and one of Connecticut's fastest-growing technology companies. Since its founding in 1984, Farmstead has grown from a small, regional remarketer of pre-owned telephone equipment to a publicly owned corporation

that has shipped $100 million worth of telephones and related equipment to more than 8,000 clients worldwide.

In 1985, AT&T named Farmstead one of its first national authorized secondary market dealers. With the restructuring of the communications giant in 1995, Farmstead joined forces with Avaya Communication, AT&T's former communications equipment operation. Together, they support the day-to-day telecommunications needs of organizations that require immediate access to Avaya equipment, rapid nationwide installation, and ongoing Avaya maintenance.

In 1998, Farmstead became one of Avaya's four Authorized Remarketing Suppliers in the United States. The company buys used telephone equipment from AT&T/Avaya, leasing companies, and end users; refurbishes it to Avaya's standards; and then re-sells it to large and small businesses, Avaya, and others. Farmstead also sells and leases new equipment.

A healthy balance sheet proves that Farmstead knows its field. From 1998 to 1999, revenue increased 19 percent to nearly $33 million. These numbers are so remarkable that in 1997, 1998, and 1999, the Connecticut Technology Council designated Farmstead a Fast 50 Company, making it one of the state's fastest-growing technology companies based on growth in revenues during the previous five years.

Whatever It Takes to Serve Customers

In the often nameless, faceless world of telecommunications, Farmstead's "whatever it takes" service philosophy sets it apart. George J. Taylor Jr., founder, chairman, and CEO, explains, "We are customer advocates, doing what very large manufacturers cannot do. We have extremely resourceful employees who are willing to go the distance for customers. So, if an order is placed by 4 p.m., we will ship it that day and dispatch an Avaya installer to appear on-site

within 48 hours. We also stock more than 40,000 Avaya parts, from the smallest printed circuit wiring assemblies to complete systems."

Customers range from television networks broadcasting major events—including political primaries, the Super Bowl, and the Olympics—to local customers with a nationwide base, such as Travelers, Aetna Inc., and United Technologies Corporation.

Farmstead's customer-friendly Internet site provides access to a buyback program, and includes a password-protected shopping catalog that is tailored to the needs of individual customers. Since 1998, Farmstead has even staffed call centers to perform sales and fulfillment functions for discontinued Spirit®, Merlin®, and older Partner® products.

Farmstead's attention to customers is nearly legendary. For two years running, the company received Avaya's Customer First Satisfaction Award for earning the highest customer satisfaction rating of all large secondary market dealers and distributors.

Farmstead's spirit of service also extends to the 16 communities where the firm has offices, and particularly to East Hartford, where most of its 145 employees work. Casual Fridays bring in contributions for a local food bank, and

employees contribute turkeys and meals during the holidays.

Taylor forecasts continued growth as the company helps clients move from voice products only to the converged world of voice, data, and Internet. Farmstead's prosperity is indicative of the firm's expertise and its devotion to customers. In little more than a decade, the company has become one of the country's premier resellers of Avaya's new, remanufactured, and refurbished business communications products and services.

THE EXECUTIVE TEAM AT FARMSTEAD TELEPHONE GROUP, INC. LEADS THE NATION'S LARGEST SUPPLIER OF BOTH REFURBISHED AND NEW AVAYA COMMUNICATION TELEPHONE PARTS. FARMSTEAD IS ONE OF CONNECTICUT'S FASTEST-GROWING TECHNOLOGY COMPANIES.

EAST HARTFORD IS THE HOME OF FARMSTEAD TELEPHONE GROUP, INC., A COMPANY THAT HAS GROWN FROM A REGIONAL REMARKETER OF PRE-OWNED TELEPHONE EQUIPMENT TO A PUBLICLY OWNED CORPORATION THAT HAS SERVED MORE THAN 8,000 CLIENTS WORLDWIDE.

Martino & Binzer

◄ WOODRUFF/BROWN

{ **M**ARTINO & BINZER IS A MARKETING AND COMMUNICATIONS firm specializing in fully integrated, innovative business-to-business (B2B) marketing programs utilizing multimedia advertising and promotion, public relations, and interactive Web development. As partners Dave Martino and Gavin Binzer tell it, that's no accident. Says Martino, agency president, }

"We're different from those agencies that see B2B as a new way to increase their billings—or to stay busy while they chase the ever elusive consumer account. Here, B2B is our life."

"We've been a B2B shop for almost 20 years now, long before it was the flavor of the day. And all that experience has endowed us with a particular kind of expertise few agencies can offer, and without which few businesses can thrive," explains Binzer.

According to Martino, "A wise old adman once told me, 'Advertising is first and foremost a business.' But I'd go a step further and say that different kinds of advertising for different kinds of businesses require different skill sets, strategies, and marketing channels. Some kinds of advertising can turn on snappy headlines and flashy graphics. Business-to-business calls for strategy first, cleverness second." Toward that end, Martino & Binzer has created a proprietary account planning methodology it calls STEP™—strategy through execution process.

AGENCY PARTNERS DAVID MARTINO AND GAVIN BINZER LEAD THE FIRM, WHICH SPECIALIZES IN FULLY INTEGRATED, INNOVATIVE BUSINESS-TO-BUSINESS MARKETING PROGRAMMING UTILIZING MULTIMEDIA ADVERTISING AND PROMOTION, PUBLIC RELATIONS, AND INTERACTIVE WEB DEVELOPMENT.

MARTINO & BINZER'S TEAM OF PROFESSIONALS COMPRISES (FROM LEFT) KIRBY, THE OFFICIAL OFFICE GREETER; DAVID MARTINO, PRESIDENT; SCOTT PORTER, ACCOUNT SERVICES DIRECTOR; MARK O'BRIEN, PUBLIC RELATIONS DIRECTOR; DAN CROCI, CREATIVE DIRECTOR; GAVIN BINZER, EXECUTIVE VICE PRESIDENT.

A STEP Ahead

STEP begins with the agency's account services, PR, media, and marketing specialists, who gather information about the client, the product, and the market. "The more information we have, the better. Ignorance may be bliss, but it doesn't generate sales," says Binzer.

Next, the agency develops strategies for branding, positioning, marketing, PR, and media placement, as well as all the tactical elements required to support those strategies. Then, and only then, does a program "go upstairs," where writers and designers, working closely with agency account executives, turn strategies into targeted communication tools such as print and broadcast ads, direct mail campaigns, communications pieces, Web sites, corporate ID, collateral brochures, and trade show graphics.

Martino & Binzer tracks the effectiveness of all marketing programs because in B2B advertising, today's hindsight is tomorrow's expertise. Given the recent proliferation of mergers, acquisitions, partnerships, alliances, distribution agreements, and e-commerce portals, that expertise is becoming increasingly vital.

"The digital age is really just the emergence of another distribution channel," says Binzer. "We've successfully harnessed the medium to help our clients establish identities,

◄ WOODRUFF/BROWN

launch brands, sell products, and promote services." Indeed, the diversity and caliber of Martino & Binzer's work are also reflected in the diversity and caliber of the agency's clients.

Over the years, Martino & Binzer has created successful promotions for a wide variety of products and services—from blenders, chemicals, hand tools, and fiber optics to industrial adhesives, gearing, insurance technology, and basketballs. The agency's clients include business and industry leaders such as Loctite Corporation, Lucent Technologies, Boston Gear, AMS Services, and Rhone-Poulenc, as well as brand-name companies such as Waring, Spalding Sports, and Reebok.

Martino & Binzer has won many effectiveness awards based on the level of readership and/or lead generation its promotional programs have produced. "Creativity is essential—but winning beauty contests isn't our goal," says Martino. "Our goal is to get our clients results, and we've been very successful at doing just that."

Results-Oriented Service

But Martino & Binzer's facility for B2B isn't the only thing that sets the agency apart. For one thing, the term "full-service" really means something at Martino & Binzer, because the agency's professionals are not simply in the business of selling ads. A broadly experienced creative and account

Easy as

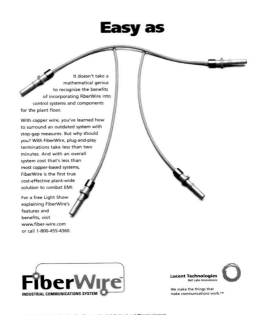

It doesn't take a mathematical genius to recognize the benefits of incorporating FiberWire into control systems and components for the plant floor.

With copper wire, you've learned how to surround an outdated system with stop-gap measures. But why should you? With FiberWire, plug-and-play terminations take less than two minutes. And with an overall system cost that's less than most copper-based systems, FiberWire is the first true cost-effective plant-wide solution to combat EMI.

For a free Light Show explaining FiberWire's features and benefits, visit www.fiber-wire.com or call 1-800-455-4360.

FiberWire™
INDUSTRIAL COMMUNICATIONS SYSTEM

Lucent Technologies
Bell Labs Innovations
We make the things that make communications work.™

Also available from Allen-Bradley, Siemens, Hewlett-Packard, and Phoenix Contact.

USING PRODUCTS AS MORE THAN JUST PHOTO PROPS, MARTINO & BINZER HELPED LUCENT TECHNOLOGIES INTRODUCE FIBER-OPTIC CABLING TO THE INDUSTRIAL MARKETPLACE (LEFT).

MUSICAL PREFERENCES ASIDE, THE AGENCY CREATED INNOVATIVE PRINT MATERIALS THAT SET THE STAGE FOR AN ANNUAL CONCERT SERIES (RIGHT).

team offers expertise in all aspects of advertising, communications, and public relations for all media.

For another thing, Martino & Binzer doesn't bill by the hour. Says Binzer, "With most agencies, they see you, and they bill you. They think about you, and they bill you. Not us. We use a phase-based, fixed-price process to estimate fees, determine timing, and define deliverables up front."

Adds Martino, "That puts the burden of profitability where it belongs—on our ability to deliver what we should, when we should. We also insist on senior-level account supervision and complete access to all personnel, ensuring knowledgeable leadership and direct communication."

"While we believe in cultivating young talent, we tend to keep the rookies in support roles till they're ready for the starting lineup." says Binzer.

Finally, the staff at Martino & Binzer is so down to earth that even the office mascot is welcome at meetings. Kirby, a handsome golden retriever/chocolate Lab, is usually found somewhere near the front door or directly beside anyone with any kind of food. Fortunately, his taste in people is less discerning. "He is the official greeter. We think there was one person he didn't like, once. But for the most part, it's one lick and you're in," says Martino.

"We try not to take ourselves too seriously. We'd rather focus on working hard for our clients," says Binzer. "We have a responsibility to offer them value."

"Measurable value," adds Martino. "After all, advertising is first and foremost a business—for us and for them."

"Essentially, we're all logical positivists with a touch of utilitarian pragmatism and some market-based savvy thrown in for good measure. In other words, we believe in results. We're not part of the art-for-art's-sake crowd. Heck, we don't even know who Art is. Besides, we're running a business here, not a museum," according to Kirby.

Hmm....I could use New DURABOND epoxies & urethanes for assembly, prototyping, rework and MRO applications – from machine tools to automotive, medical and electrical equipment. DURABOND structural adhesives can help me out of a lot of sticky situations.

NOW, THE ONLY THING WE CAN'T HOLD IS A SECRET.

GET A FREE SAMPLE OF NEW DURABOND STRUCTURAL ADHESIVES - ONLY FROM LOCTITE.

HEARD THE LATEST BUZZ ABOUT LOCTITE – AND STRUCTURAL ADHESIVES? WE WANTED YOU TO HEAR ABOUT IT FROM US FIRST. IT'S DURABOND – A NEW HIGH PERFORMANCE PRODUCT LINE WITH 12 EPOXIES AND 2 URETHANES. AND THE WHOLE LINE IS BACKED BY LOCTITE TECHNOLOGY WITH HIGH-STRENGTH, DURABILITY, AND A WIDE RANGE OF CURE TIMES. BUT THE LATEST WORD IS – CUSTOM FORMULATIONS. TRY TO GET THAT OUT OF ANYONE BUT LOCTITE.

Call 1-800-323-0108 ext. 42 or visit our website at www.loctite.com/durabond to get the whole story on DURABOND – and receive a FREE sample delivered right to your door by your local Loctite representative.

FREE SAMPLE

LOCTITE
TECHNOLOGY BEYOND THE BOTTLE.

THE
beauty
is in the **details.**

We've been in the best kitchens for over 60 years. But it's our details – gorgeous color palette, timeless quality, and elegant lines, that keep us out of the cabinets and on the countertops. Call 1-800-4WARING for the retailer nearest you.

WARING
269 Main Street, New Hartford, CT 06057

USING A UNIQUE SPIN ON WORD-OF-MOUTH ADVERTISING FOR LOCTITE CORPORATION, MARTINO & BINZER SHOWCASED ONE OF CONNECTICUT'S PREMIER HOMEGROWN COMPANIES (LEFT).

WITH THE CLASSIC STYLING AND TIMELESS BEAUTY OF ITS PRODUCTS, THE AGENCY'S WORK DEMONSTRATED THAT WARING HAS SOMETHING NO OTHER BLENDER MANUFACTURER COULD OFFER (RIGHT).

Rome McGuigan Sabanosh, P.C.

ROME McGuigan Sabanosh, P.C. enjoys an enviable niche among Connecticut law firms. At 20 years old, the firm is forward thinking and entrepreneurial, recognizing that success is determined by a reputation for solving problems and delivering value, rather than by generational ties. The firm's 20 principals' average of 20 years in practice provides the optimum blend of energy and experience,

ROME McGuigan Sabanosh, P.C. ENTERS ITS THIRD DECADE WITH UN- BRIDLED ENTHUSIASM AND A DEEP- ROOTED RESPECT AND APPRECIATION FOR THE PROFESSION AND THE OPPORTUNITIES AHEAD.

allowing them to be hands-on in responding to their clients' needs. The firm recognizes that, as corporate clients have shortened their outside counsel lists, Rome McGuigan Sabanosh has remained a preferred provider of services due to its high-quality product; responsive, timely service; flexibility in addressing the client's pricing and billing objectives; and sensitivity to the client's need for up-to-date information.

The creative, results-oriented approach Rome McGuigan applies to every client engagement is enhanced by the substantial government, business, and community experience many of its lawyers

bring to the firm. Whether performing key roles in the public sector as government prosecutors, including a former chief state's attorney and a former chief trial attorney for the states' attorney's office; serving as a leader in the state legislature; or chairing or serving on the boards of many of the state's most respected charitable, political, educational, and health care institutions, the principals of the firm have provided leadership and substantial contributions to the functions and vitality of the state, independent of their roles in the law firm. This experience enables the firm to bring a broader understanding of government, the judicial process,

and business to the legal counsel and representation it provides clients.

Diverse Areas of Expertise

Rome McGuigan Sabanosh specializes in civil and commercial litigation in all courts; corporate; commercial finance; real estate; employment; labor law; intellectual property; trade secrets litigation; product liability litigation; Indian gaming; municipal and corporate investigations; personal injury; matrimonial law; white-collar criminal defense; tax advocacy and business; and tax and estate planning. The firm's main office is in Hartford, and the labor and employment group is based in Bridgeport.

With several former prosecutors among its principals, it is no surprise that litigation is the firm's largest practice area. The members of the firm understand, however, that there are times when excellent litigation skills alone are not enough: that businesses and municipalities are being victimized from both within and outside their organizations, often requiring expert investigative research and strategies. The firm has a team of attorneys experienced in conducting investigations who maintain a close working relationship with prosecutors and law enforcement agencies in Connecticut and throughout the country. Their investigative efforts have resulted in the arrest, conviction, and incarceration of individuals who have misappropriated proprietary information, computer technology, industrial materials, and other property. The firm's experience in managing complex and sensitive investigations and its working relationships with investigators throughout the United States enables it to insulate the client from, and reduce the risk of, liability to third parties. Rome McGuigan Sabanosh takes pride in having resolved some of its most difficult cases prior to engaging in costly and uncertain litigation, and recognizes

◀ JEFFREY YARDIS

that a confidential settlement agreement is often the best way to resolve sensitive security breaches.

The firm's corporate and finance attorneys have been representing corporations, developers, and financial institutions for more than 20 years with a commitment to anticipating and resolving complications before they adversely impact a transaction. This approach allowed the firm to successfully close the first public offering for a Native American tribe on Wall Street in 1995. It also placed the firm at the forefront of the current revitalization of Hartford.

The tax advocacy group at Rome McGuigan Sabanosh assists taxpayers at all levels in dealing with taxing authorities who are aggressively interpreting and enforcing tax laws and regulations as their state and local governments grapple with increasing costs of services and budget constraints. The firm's representation of individual and corporate clients in matters involving allegations of criminal tax fraud is enhanced significantly by those of its attorneys who have served previously as government prosecutors.

Being entrepreneurial themselves, members of the business and tax planning group at the firm appreciate that business owners and their families require a special blend of legal services from experienced lawyers who are able to assess their individual personal and business needs with care, and successfully guide the business owner through the various stages of building a business and accumulating and preserving personal assets.

The attorneys in the labor and employment group work to under-

stand the client's business and its strategic plan to assist management in achieving its goals. They recognize that the vigorous defense of claims and suits filed against the client creates leverage for negotiation of favorable settlements, but that the objective is, whenever possible, to enable the client to concentrate on furthering its business interests and statutory responsibilities, instead of expending resources in defense of claims and suits.

Professional Development and Prestige

The attorneys at Rome McGuigan Sabanosh actively participate in many professional associations in and outside of Connecticut. Members of the firm have served as members of the National Board of Trial Advocacy; panels of arbitrators for both the American Arbitration Association and Dispute Resolution, Inc.; the National District Attorneys Asso-

ciation; the board of the American Prosecutors Research Institute; the Connecticut Defense Attorneys Association; the Defense Research Institute; the Association of Trial Lawyers of America; and the Connecticut Criminal Defense Lawyers Association. The firm's attorneys have also served as executive director of the Council on Probate, special counsel to the Connecticut Statewide Grievance Committee, special master of the superior court, and president-elect of the Hartford County Bar Association. The firm encourages this involvement and recognizes that the reputations of its members are heightened by these activities.

Rome McGuigan Sabanosh, P.C. enters its third decade with unbridled enthusiasm and a deep-rooted respect and appreciation for the profession and the opportunities ahead.

ROME MCGUIGAN SABANOSH HAS REMAINED A PREFERRED PROVIDER OF SERVICES DUE TO ITS HIGH-QUALITY PRODUCT; RESPONSIVE, TIMELY SERVICE; FLEXIBILITY IN ADDRESSING THE CLIENT'S PRICING AND BILLING OBJECTIVES; AND SENSITIVITY TO THE CLIENT'S NEED FOR UP-TO-DATE INFORMATION.

The Allied Group Inc.

I N THE DYNAMIC SOFTWARE AND HIGH-TECHNOLOGY INDUSTRY THAT IS reshaping Connecticut's economic landscape, the Allied Group Inc. is an innovative company that designs, develops, and deploys advanced e-business applications and infrastructures for clients ranging from Fortune 1000 companies to dot-coms. ❋ The Allied Group was founded in 1984 to serve the engineering and technical computer workstation market,

but over time, realized that while profitable, this business offered limited possibilities for growth. The company's decision to change course—to support client-server technology in the commercial marketplace by designing and implementing enterprise infrastructures—has made it one of the fastest-growing technology companies in the country.

In 1994, the U.S Small Business Administration (SBA) gave the Allied Group a loan to aid in its development efforts. At that time, the company had 15 employees and $4.3 million in revenue, and was in a single office in Glastonbury. Just five years later, the firm closed 1999 with some $110 million in revenue, more than 200 employees, and locations along the eastern seaboard from Boston to Richmond.

Such explosive growth has not gone unnoticed. The Allied Group was named to the Deloitte & Touche Fast 500 list of the fastest-growing U.S. technology companies, and was named to *Inc.* magazine's list of the 500 fastest-growing U.S. private companies. The SBA gave Irvin Miglietta,

Allied's president and CEO, its Entrepreneurial Success Award, which honors the most innovative and successful entrepreneurs across the nation. In Connecticut, the company ranked 10th on the Deloitte & Touche/Connecticut Technology Council Fast 50 list. Recently, because he best embodies the spirit of Connecticut by promoting the state as a great place to do business,

Miglietta was named the recipient of the You Belong in Connecticut business contest sponsored by the Connecticut Economic Resource Center (CERC), Star 99.9 WEZN, and the Connecticut Radio Network.

Secrets of Success

The Allied Group's impressive accomplishments are rooted in its clear vision, well-defined methodologies, partnerships with best-of-breed Internet technology vendors, and unparalleled technical excellence.

"The Allied Group helps companies evolve wisely in the changing tides of technology," says Miglietta. "Nearly every industry is undergoing revolutionary changes fueled by the capabilities of Internet technologies and driven by the potential of e-business economics. We're in the business of connecting people in an efficient, intelligent, and profitable way."

Today's race to use technology for profit potential is acting as an unprecedented catalyst in business transformation. This race creates tremendous opportunity for Internet professional services companies such as the Allied Group. And because of this rapid change in the industry, the Allied Group maintains strong relationships with leading Internet technology vendors, including Sun Microsystems, Oracle Corporation,

AN INNOVATIVE COMPANY THAT DESIGNS, DEVELOPS, AND DEPLOYS ADVANCED E-BUSINESS APPLICATIONS, THE ALLIED GROUP INC. SERVES CLIENTS RANGING FROM FORTUNE 1000 COMPANIES TO DOT-COMS.

Cisco Systems, and Veritas Software. These partners, who see Allied as a strategic leader and innovator, give it first-in-line access to new technologies and privileged information, as well as the highest level of certification for employees.

The Allied Group's reputation for technical excellence is enhanced by its commitment to providing extensive professional training not only to employees, but to clients as well. The training delivered through Allied University—the only Authorized Sun Education Center in the state of Connecticut—reflects the company's desire to deliver a totally integrated solution to its clients and to provide employees with the highest level of education available. The Allied Group offers professional classes and certification programs that help individuals maximize their productivity and increase their competitive advantage.

Helping Clients Prosper

The Allied Group measures its successes by those of its clients, who demonstrate their satisfaction through their continued trust and long-term partnerships with the company. The Allied Group prides itself in evolving wisely to leverage the technologies of the future. The company's services and methodologies enable it to provide clients with timely and complete solutions that advance clients' business initiatives and give them a competitive advantage. And the Allied Group's history of delivering advanced technology solutions on time

and within budget illustrates mastery of the firm's core competencies.

According to David Campana, manager of application development at Tech Republic, a subsidiary of the Gartner Group, "With the Allied Group's overall presence and expertise, we really hit the nail on the head. They gave us prompt attention, met tight deadlines, and exemplified great teamwork. We couldn't have asked for anything more."

Another client, Stephen Gloyd, senior vice president of sales for American Petroleum Exchange, says, "The Allied Group's expertise and guidance are instrumental to our business plan."

Referring to the Allied Group's innovative business solution for Otis Elevator, Dr. Bruce A. Powell, Otis Technical Fellow, says, "On very rare occasions during a working career of more than 30 years, a project comes along which has a mysterious, magical quality. What makes the magic is interpersonal chemistry, which is hard to quantify. The Web OtisPlan project has been such a project for me."

Supporting Youth and Education

The Allied Group and its employees demonstrate a strong commitment to youth and education through community involvement. The only technology company to sponsor the University of Connecticut's athletic program, the firm also helps sponsor Connecticut Public Television's Family Science Expo, the Greater

Hartford Marathon, and the Manchester Road Race. The company and its employees contribute to organizations such as the American Cancer Society and the Make-a-Wish Foundation, mentor local schoolchildren, and volunteer at local events such as the Canon Greater Hartford Open and the American Cancer Society's Run for Life.

As it enters an era that will present unprecedented opportunities, the Allied Group plans to flourish as it has for 15 years by nurturing long-term relationships and understanding that evolution—especially in technology—is a never ending process.

Tallán, Inc.

WITH EXPERIENCE IN EMERGING TECHNOLOGIES, AN outstanding roster of world-class clients, and an especially rich base of talent, Tallán, Inc. is a leader in the e-business arena. The company delivers Internet and e-commerce services such as data warehousing, data mining, and on-line transaction processing systems to Global 2000

corporations and large dot-com companies, including Priceline.com, Best Buy, Columbia House, Wit Capital, eToys, and Barnes & Noble.

Tallán is one of the fastest-growing technology companies in the United States. In 1999, it was number 225 on Deloitte & Touche's Fast 500 list, made *Inc.* magazine's Inc. 500 list for the third consecutive year, and was named a Fast 50 company by the Connecticut Technology Council for the second straight year.

The company's story of success is impressive, even in the lightning-fast world of Internet-related business. Founded in 1985 as Business Data Services (BDS), the family-owned company developed customized e-business systems and software for small companies. The firm quickly gained a knack for developing systems using the most advanced technologies, and excelled at applications that had complex, distributed architectures. BDS was working in networked distributed systems and Unix in the mid-1980s, long before other developers.

AT THE HELM OF TALLÁN, INC. ARE CEO JACK HUGHES AND COO ROB HUGHES (TOP).

TALLÁN'S PHENOMENAL SUCCESS CAN BE ATTRIBUTED DIRECTLY TO ITS EMPLOYEES—THE TALENT THAT IS THE STRENGTH OF THE BUSINESS (BOTTOM).

As the company gained experience and its reputation spread in the early days of Internet development, revenue grew briskly. BDS brought in $13 million in 1997, $22 million in 1998, and, after significantly adding to its client base, earned $53 million in 1999.

In mid-1999, the company brought about the most significant change in its history when it approached Andover-based CMGI, Inc. to become a client. CMGI—the world's largest and most diverse network of Internet companies—was impressed enough to buy a majority interest in the firm and completed the agreement in April 2000. Now, with the resources of its new parent company, Tallán can offer its customers excellent potential in the global business-to-business marketplace. Though its headquarters, recruiting, client management, and sales management offices remain in Glastonbury, additional offices are located throughout the United States.

Top Talent, Top Clients, Top-Notch Success

Jack Hughes, cofounder and CEO, attributes the phenomenal success of the Glastonbury company to the strength of its employees. He talks about a "virtuous circle" whereby top technical talent attracts top clients,

who in turn attract additional talented recruits, who then attract more world-class business, and so on. In January 2000, Hughes even renamed his company Tallán—a Gaelic word for talent—as a tribute to employees and a reflection of its talent-centric business strategy.

Recognizing that its talent is the company's sole source of revenue, 12 full-time technical recruiters conduct a rigorous search for talented and driven consultants, designers, developers, and engineers. At Tallán, all members of each project team interact directly with the company's clients on challenging and exciting projects using state-of-the-art technology. Employees frequently work long hours, but are regularly recognized and rewarded for their contributions.

As new and existing clients have demanded more services, the company has significantly increased its workforce. After hiring more than 150 people in 1999, Tallán doubled again in 2000. Of the firm's more than 600 employees, more than 80 percent are revenue producing. In addition to developers, there are employees in sales, marketing, recruiting and human resources, accounting and finance, in-house technical support, and administration. As a result of Tallán's demanding

recruiting process and the opportunities and rewards it offers, Tallán, Inc. has an annual attrition rate of about 15 percent, versus an industry average of 30 percent.

Giving Clients Competitive Advantage

Tallán employees are devoted to applying new technologies to clients' competitive advantage. They deliver a framework of leading-edge e-business solutions customized to the clients' needs, but adaptable to future opportunities.

Tallán also brings to its clients a unique project methodology. Where the industry typically uses a fixed-cost approach to implementation and budgeting, the company's project-based system breaks down every aspect of the plan, building it in segments to gain the flexibility and speed needed to exceed expectations.

When Priceline.com envisioned a revolutionary Web site where customers could name their own price for groceries, it turned to Tallán. In just four months of collaboration, Tallán had created the entire system and Web site, including a complex decisioning engine and support systems for customer service, credit card authorization, debit card payment processing, and customer promotions. Priceline WebHouse Club has sold more than 1 million items from its more than 150 product categories.

With iSolve, Tallán built a Web site that brings together buyers and sellers throughout the world, and changes the way surplus goods are bought and sold. Using next-generation technology, Tallán developed the site using a three-tier architecture; designed a Web-based customer service tool used to administer customer accounts and listings, and to track customer calls; built a reporting capability to track Web usage and customer activity; designed the system hardware architecture; and built iSolve's company network infrastructure.

The company also developed enhanced software applications for Fiera.com, Inc., a Spanish language e-commerce site for Latin Americans and U.S. Hispanics. Fiera.com's varied product mix includes computers, books, toys, and cosmetics. Tallán's best-of-breed applications will provide Fiera.com with the flexibility it requires for new products and services.

With its valuable combination of superb talent and experience in advanced technologies, Tallán is well equipped to expand on its rich heritage in the increasingly competitive and fast-paced Internet industry.

Familymeds, Inc.

FAMILYMEDS, INC., FORMERLY KNOWN AS ARROW PHARMACY & NUTRITION CENTERS, COMBINES THE TRADITIONAL ARROW PHARMACIES WITH AN INTERNET STORE TO TRANSCEND ITS STATUS AS A REGIONAL CHAIN AND BECOME AMERICA'S MEDICATION SPECIALIST.

SINCE ITS BEGINNING, ARROW PHARMACY & NUTRITION CENTERS HAS focused solely on the pharmaceutical health of its customers. From operating pharmacies in conjunction with hospitals and medical offices to training its pharmacists in nutrition and herbal treatments, Arrow prides itself on being a complete health and nutrition company, rather than just a local drugstore. Now, with the advent of the

Internet, Arrow has amended its more traditional bricks-and-mortar operation with the launching of Familymeds.com, a full-service on-line pharmacy and health Web site.

The Arrow Corporation was established in 1987 with five franchised pharmacies in Connecticut. From the outset, Arrow eschewed the drugstore extras in favor of a store devoted strictly to health. The franchises don't sell cigarettes, make-up, or school supplies; instead of these items, they feature a knowledgeable staff and a complete line of herbal remedies, vitamins, and nutritional supplements.

This emphasis has clearly worked. Initially, customer response was so enthusiastic that, by 1998, Arrow had 71 pharmacies in supermarkets and hospitals, as well as freestanding retail sites in six states. By January 2000, the company had expanded to include 122 pharmacies in 15 states, reporting annualized revenues of $250 million for 1999. Today, it is one of the top 20 retail pharmacy operators in the country.

Arrow, now known as Familymeds, Inc., combines the traditional Arrow pharmacies with an Internet store to transcend its status as a regional chain and become America's medication specialist. Pharmacist Ed Mercadante envisions a continuum of health care among doctors, pharmacies, and the Internet in which patients visit the doctor, fill a prescription on-site, and then log on to the Internet for ongoing refills, nonprescription products, and health care information and recommendations. As president and CEO of Familymeds, Mercadante is blending a tradition of old-fashioned service with new technologies to make that dream a reality.

Even as the company experiences phenomenal growth, Familymeds pharmacies continue to be known for customer service and for the education and information of patients. Pharmacists are trained and certified in nutrition; the stores

▼ JEFF YARDIS

offer a comprehensive line of vitamins, herbs, and homeopathic remedies. Familymeds pharmacists even make house calls, so to speak. Within 48 hours of filling a prescription for a child, they call the family to ensure that the medication is being taken properly and that the child is showing improvement.

Putting Pharmacy Services a Click Away

Mercadante believes that while people will continue to rely on drugstores to fill prescriptions for acute illnesses, many will go on-line for maintenance medications, used to treat chronic conditions such as blood pressure and cholesterol drugs; vitamins; and health and beauty aids. Indeed, industry analysts predict that on-line pharmacies—offering convenience, easy access to information, wide selections, low prices, and around-the-clock service—are expected to be a $2.4 billion business by 2003.

Companies that can provide both virtual and traditional drugstores

will have a distinct advantage. With more than 100,000 customers a month, Familymeds.com has become one of the fastest-growing pharmacy Web sites on the Internet. Sales grew exponentially to more than $5 million in June 2000, and the company expects that rate of growth to continue through 2000.

Familymeds.com offers prescription medicines and more than 30,000 over-the-counter health and beauty products, vitamins and herbal supplements, personal care products, medical provisions, and other remedies. Familymeds.com approximates the personalized services and advice that people experience in the company's retail stores. A team of on-line pharmacists provides a personal touch by being available via e-mail and phone 24 hours a day, seven days a week, to answer customer questions and make recommendations.

On-Line Health Clinics

To make educated decisions about their health, Familymeds customers also can obtain education and

▲ JEFF YARDIS

▲ JEFF YARDIS

EVEN AS THE COMPANY EXPERIENCES
PHENOMENAL GROWTH, FAMILYMEDS
PHARMACIES CONTINUE TO BE KNOWN
FOR CUSTOMER SERVICE AND FOR
THE EDUCATION AND INFORMATION
IT PROVIDES TO PATIENTS.

information from more than 250 on-line health clinics. They can visit the asthma clinic, for example, and learn about asthma's causes, symptoms, diagnosis, and treatment; see the pharmacist's recommendations for which medications help specific aspects of asthma most effectively; and get advice about nonprescription treatments and nutritional approaches. Customers can print the information and use it while consulting with their physician. Working with its pharmacists, the company continues to add additional features to its Web site.

Although Familymeds.com shoppers often receive their maintenance prescriptions by mail, they have the option of same-day pickup of acute care and maintenance drugs at a Familymeds pharmacy or a participating pharmacy in a network of more than 4,400 independent pharmacies.

"Our Internet concept allows patients to access more information while removing barriers to compliance," Mercadante says. "This technology will provide the means to connect physicians, pharmacists, and consumers, resulting in better-coordinated health care." He is confident that this specialized approach will set Familymeds.com apart in the increasingly active on-line marketplace. A recent study by *e-Marketer*, a leading on-line business publication, supports his view, ranking the site one of the top five on-line drugstores.

Familymeds' combination of increasing its bricks-and-mortar locations and enhancing its Internet operation is backed by conventional marketing partnerships as well. Through a partnership with Centrus Pharmacy Solutions, a pharmacy benefits manager based in Albany, New York, Familymeds has a custom Web site for Centrus' managed care and employer clients, as well as its co-branded marketing materials. Familymeds also has relationships with TheSeniorNetwork.com, Complexions Rx, Homecare America, and BioTherapies, Inc. to offer on-line consumers a combination of products and expert advice.

With a proud heritage of patient care, additional planned acquisitions, and a successful Internet store, Familymeds, Inc. has begun to realize its vision of drug retailing in the 21st century—a fully integrated pharmaceutical and nutraceutical consumer delivery system that will help people lead healthy lives.

FAMILYMEDS.COM OFFERS PRES-
CRIPTION MEDICINES AND MORE
THAN 30,000 OVER-THE-COUNTER
HEALTH AND BEAUTY PRODUCTS,
VITAMINS AND HERBAL SUPPLE-
MENTS, PERSONAL CARE PRODUCTS,
MEDICAL PROVISIONS, AND OTHER
REMEDIES.

{1990–2001}

1990   CARRIER CORPORATION

1990   THE MAGEE MARKETING GROUP, INC.

1992   HARTFORD BUSINESS JOURNAL

1992   JDS UNIPHASE ELECTRO-OPTIC PRODUCTS DIVISION

1992   OPEN SOLUTIONS INC.

1994   SMITH WHILEY & COMPANY

1996   CONNECTICUT CHILDREN'S MEDICAL CENTER

1996   OEM OF CONNECTICUT, INC.

1997   CB RICHARD ELLIS - N.E. PARTNERS, LP

1999   PERMATEX, INC.

Carrier Corporation

WHETHER THEY ARE TOURING THE WORLD'S LARGEST COVered entertainment space, the Millennium Dome in Greenwich, England; riding on Korea's high-speed trains; viewing Michelangelo's magnificent frescoes in the Sistine Chapel; learning about pop music legends at the Rock and Roll Hall of Fame & Museum; or just relaxing in their

own homes, people want to be comfortable when it gets too hot or too cool outside. Whatever they're doing and wherever they are, chances are that if they are enjoying a comfortable indoor climate, Carrier Corporation—the world's largest manufacturer of air-conditioning, heating, and refrigeration equipment—is responsible.

Carrier Corporation: The Father of Air-Conditioning

Although the company is known for creating custom-made indoor weather and a world of comfort, air-conditioning actually was created to cool machines, not people. Willis Carrier, an engineer, invented the basics of modern air-conditioning in 1902 to help a Brooklyn printer whose color reproductions were running due to changes in humidity and temperature.

When cotton mill owners said they couldn't work in dry buildings because the threads snapped too often, Carrier came to the rescue. He was able to control the cotton mills' temperature and humidity, which was called "conditioning" the cotton, and the name air-conditioning stuck. For the next two decades, Carrier helped other manufacturers. Eventually, movie theaters and deluxe hotels used air-conditioning to attract business, and the modern-day industry was born.

Almost 100 years after its founding, the company offers a multitude of air-conditioning, heating, and refrigeration products that range from compact window room air conditioners only eight inches high to large-capacity chillers for skyscrapers, commercial trade centers, and domed sports arenas. Carrier Corporation products include air-handling units, compressors, condensers, hermetic absorption and centrifugal water chillers, dehumidifiers, electronic control systems, air cleaners, and more.

Hundreds of distributors and thousands of dealers sell, install,

▲ LANNY NAGLER

CARRIER CORPORATION'S WORLD HEADQUARTERS, LOCATED IN FARMINGTON, CONNECTICUT, IS HOME BASE FOR CARRIER'S PRESIDENT AND NEARLY 200 EXECUTIVES, MANAGERS, AND STAFF.

and service Carrier Corporation products in more than 170 countries. The company's products are designed and engineered in 20 centers and manufactured in 70 facilities spread across six continents.

Carrier Corporation continues to expand its global reach through an aggressive acquisition strategy. In 1999, the firm had more than 40,000 employees worldwide and revenue that exceeded $7.4 billion.

Protecting the Environment

In keeping with its unsurpassed global presence, and in the tradition of Willis Carrier, the company is an innovator. In 1994, Carrier Corporation began phasing out ozone-depleting refrigerants and became

the first heating, ventilation, and air-conditioning company with a line of environmentally friendly products.

Puron™ is Carrier Corporation's brand name for the first chlorine-free, non-ozone-depleting refrigerant for residential air-conditioning systems. Not only is Puron environmentally sound, but it also offers high efficiency and long-term cost savings. Carrier Corporation considers this revolutionary creation to be essential to the future of the heating and cooling industry.

The company's next major foray will be the Internet. According to Jon Ayers, president, "Carrier Corporation must embrace the unprecedented business opportunity to redefine our E-business and provide

CARRIER EQUIPMENT MAINTAINS THE INTEGRITY OF THE GREAT SENATE CHAMBER, PART OF THE RECENTLY RENOVATED OLD STATE HOUSE IN HARTFORD. THE 350-YEAR-OLD BUILDING HAS WITNESSED MAJOR EVENTS IN CONNECTICUT'S HISTORY, SUCH AS THE MOMENTOUS AMISTAD TRIAL.

higher levels of customer satisfaction and value." Ayers says E-business provides an opportunity to reduce costs and non-value-added activity, and will allow the company to effectively manage and share knowledge internally and collaborate on a global scale. Carrier Corporation's E-business efforts also will support development of strategies to build customer demand, and integrate existing marketing channels and suppliers globally.

Practicing Good Citizenship

Since 1990, Carrier Corporation's world headquarters has been located in the Hartford area, which is also the home of its parent company, United Technologies Corporation

(UTC). In addition to Carrier Corporation air-conditioning units, UTC's lineup of famous products includes Otis elevators, Pratt & Whitney aircraft engines, Sikorsky helicopters, and Hamilton Sundstrand aerospace systems.

Carrier Corporation and its employees are committed to the vitality of the capital city. The company provided major heating and air-conditioning restoration for the Hill-Stead Museum in Farmington, preserving its French impressionist masterpieces for years to come. In 1999, Carrier Corporation donated air-conditioning to the Connecticut Audubon Center in Glastonbury, ensuring the comfort of its visitors and animals.

In 1998 and 1999, employees joined with Trinity College to build two homes in Hartford through Habitat for Humanity, an organization that the company supports worldwide. Carrier Corporation's American employees have helped build 26 homes in nine locations, and the Asia Pacific office has built 10 houses in a Manila suburb.

With UTC, Carrier Corporation sponsors Hartford's annual Symphony on Ice, and regularly hosts the exciting Grand Prix "mini-Indy" race in downtown Hartford as a fund-raiser for Junior Achievement.

As its employees revitalize their communities and its product line enjoys success throughout the world, Carrier Corporation continues to make important contributions to the way people live, work, and play.

CLOCKWISE FROM TOP LEFT: AT THE CHEK LAP KOK AIRPORT IN HONG KONG, CARRIER PROVIDES RELIEF FROM THE HEAT TO 35 MILLION AIRLINE PASSENGERS.

CARRIER COOLS KOREA'S DAEWOO HIGH-SPEED TRAINS THAT WILL CARRY MORE THAN 100 MILLION PASSENGERS A YEAR.

IN 1999, EMPLOYEES FROM THE CARRIER HEADQUARTERS, ALONG WITH TRINITY COLLEGE, BUILT THE COMPANY'S SECOND HABITAT HOUSE IN HARTFORD.

TWENTY-FOUR CARRIER CHILLERS COOLED THE MILLENNIUM DOME, THE WORLD'S LARGEST ENTERTAINMENT COMPLEX, IN GREENWICH, ENGLAND.

The Magee Marketing Group, Inc.

SINCE 1990, THE MAGEE MARKETING GROUP, INC. HAS PROVIDED FULL-service advertising, marketing, and public relations services while proving there's truth in the old saying that good things come in small packages. With fewer than 10 full- and part-time employees, the agency has served many of the Hartford area's largest, most successful, and best-known companies, including Travelers, The Hartford, Aetna,

IN 1998, THE MAGEE MARKETING GROUP, INC. BOUGHT AND RENOVATED A BUILDING IN OLD WETHERSFIELD, RECEIVING THE TOWN'S TOP ECONOMIC DEVELOPMENT AND IMPROVEMENT AWARD IN THE PROCESS.

Northeast Utilities, Kaman Industrial Technologies, Superior Electric, Barden Corporation, Scan-Optics, Hamar Laser, and ADC Telecommunications.

Brian Magee, founder and president, explains that maintaining a small staff reduces overhead and gives him the flexibility to retain skilled people as needed. "Today, most companies demand a lean approach to doing business," he says. "While we do a national-level job in terms of quality, we don't charge national-level prices. The companies we work with recognize this fact and appreciate our efforts to keep costs in line."

Yankee Work Ethic

A 30-year marketing veteran, Magee says the entrepreneurial bug bit him in 1990, after two decades of working mostly at other advertising agencies. He turned several rooms in his Wethersfield home into incubator space and, with $5,000 in start-up capital, got to work. Magee hired his first employee within three months, and ended the first year with 12 clients and $257,000 in gross revenues. With business growing, despite a deep recession, The Magee Marketing Group added employees and moved to larger, leased office space in 1992. By 1997, revenues had climbed to $647,000. At this point, the agency made a strategic shift in focus to concentrate on serving fewer, but larger, business-to-business clients. The move was clearly the right one, since earnings soared. By 1998, annual billings were $6 million.

Today, The Magee Marketing Group enjoys a well-deserved reputation for providing companies with a range of innovative marketing communications solutions. Services include strategic planning, research, media analysis and placement, advertising, public relations, graphic design and production, video, and Web site and e-business development.

Magee says, "We are not the biggest, the wealthiest, the splashiest, or even the oldest advertising agency in Connecticut. But, like our New England ancestors, we work extremely hard and take quiet pride in our many accomplishments."

Rules of Engagement

Magee is quick to note that clients are at the heart of day-to-day life at The Magee Marketing Group. Fast, responsive client service is one of the agency's "rules of engagement," which support its mission to help companies do a better job of marketing their products and services.

"Our existence is predicated

FOR 10 YEARS, THE FIRM HAS SERVED MANY OF THE HARTFORD AREA'S LARGEST, MOST SUCCESSFUL, AND BEST-KNOWN COMPANIES.

Magee Marketing Group to make a major investment in 1998. The firm bought and completely renovated a two-story, brick office building located in the Historic District of Old Wethersfield. Besides offices and meeting space, the building now houses the agency's digital photo studio, with additional space to allow for future expansion.

In 2001, Magee has plans to transform a second building on the property behind the company's main offices into a larger digital photo studio to support the agency's direct marketing, public relations, and e-business imaging needs. The annex will also house a focus group facility, along with additional production and creative work space.

In 1999, the Town of Wethersfield gave The Magee Marketing Group its top Economic Development and Improvement Award for the agency's overall contribution to economic growth and development within the community.

Entering its second decade, The Magee Marketing Group expects to expand its role of serving smart, growth-oriented companies. By abiding by Magee's three principles of success—"Work hard, work even harder, and work harder still"—the agency demonstrates its dedication to the success of its clients and proves that its reputation is well deserved in the industry.

MAGEE MARKETING NOW OPERATES ITS OWN DIGITAL PHOTO STUDIO TO SUPPORT ITS DIRECT MARKETING, PUBLIC RELATIONS, AND E-BUSINESS IMAGING NEEDS.

solely on successfully selling our clients' products, ideas, and services," says Magee. "We set high performance standards for ourselves and we consistently offer practical solutions that are sensitive to client needs and limitations. We remain flexible enough to respond quickly to changing market conditions."

The Magee Marketing Group utilizes an agency-developed, proprietary strategic planning process. This comprehensive, copyrighted approach involves a series of progressive steps that begin with a market research, situation analysis, and problem definition phase, and continue through to strategic, tactical execution, budgeting, and monitoring phases. The agency's

methodology received critical acclaim by a national agency management group, and permission was granted for use of this planning tool by other agencies in non-competing markets.

Respect, honesty, and ethical conduct are important agency qualities. "Vendors in particular enjoy working with us because they know they will be treated with the utmost respect," says Magee. He adds that the agency is fiscally conservative and always charges a fair, reasonable price for its services.

New Home, New Possibilities

Hard work has led to satisfied clients, record billings, and exceptional profits, which in turn allowed The

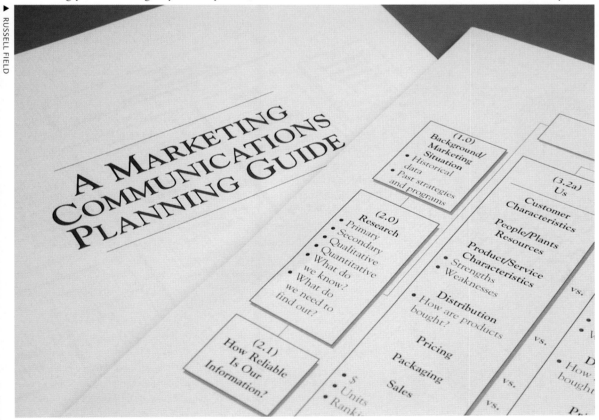

A MARKETING COMMUNICATIONS PLANNING GUIDE

THE AGENCY DEVELOPED A PROPRIETARY STRATEGIC PLANNING PROCESS THAT HAS RECEIVED CRITICAL ACCLAIM BY A NATIONAL AGENCY MANAGEMENT GROUP.

Hartford
Business Journal

T HE *Hartford Business Journal* IS THE LEADING SOURCE OF LOCAL BUSINESS news in Hartford and central Connecticut. The newspaper balances local business news with comprehensive specialty and resource publications, intended expressly for area entrepreneurs and decision makers. ✳ Giving business leaders a keener understanding of the local business environment is a key part of the *Journal*'s mission. Success in this area has

made the *Hartford Business Journal* an indispensable part of the professional lives of entrepreneurs and senior managers throughout Greater Hartford.

Being a true business resource means staying in touch with the vibrant pulse of commerce. The *Journal* produces specialty and resource publications, such as the *Fact Book,* which provides demographic facts and figures on the market, and the annual *Book of Lists,* which showcases a variety of business lists that rank numerous segments of the economy. Also, the *Journal* focuses on major local industries, as well as thriving subregional economies, within its distribution area.

Steady Growth and Progress

Started in November 1992, the *Hartford Business Journal* began with big

plans. "We had the idea of starting a business magazine in Hartford, but at that time, the area was in the midst of a serious recession. Companies were downsizing left and right, and many people really questioned our timing," says Publisher Joe Zwiebel.

The team was confident that the capital city of one of the wealthiest states in the nation and its surrounding region would have a bright future, and they plunged forward. "We knew Hartford would come back strong, and it has," Zwiebel says. "Today, the success of the *Hartford Business Journal* parallels the rebirth and renaissance in the region that the *Journal* has both reported on and been a part of since the early 1990s."

With support from both readers and advertisers, the publication has made bold changes recently. In 1996, its frequency was doubled from a biweekly to a weekly schedule to give readers more up-to-the-minute business information. The following year, the publication converted from controlled to paid circulation. In 1999, it had an estimated readership of more than 30,000, with revenues rising sharply, posting yearly increases typically in double digits.

Earning National Recognition

In addition to a strong reputation for excellence within the Hartford

area, the *Journal* has won accolades on a national level. The Association of Area Business Publications (AABP) recognized the publication for best cover for 1996 and best editorial for 1997, as well as a second place for best local spin on a national news story. In 1998, the newspaper won second honors for explanatory journalism for its series on urban comebacks. A number of these honors were in open categories, with the *Journal* competing against and winning out over strong organizations in major markets.

Much of the *Journal*'s success is attributable to its strong staff in the editorial area, as well as in sales, marketing, subscription, art, and administration. In the newsroom and throughout the organization, senior managers at the top of their careers team up with talented junior publishing professionals to produce an incisive and vibrant weekly business publication. For readers, the result is a useful tool; for advertisers, the benefit is access to an expanding business-to-business market they cannot reach as effectively through any other local media.

Change is a given in the news business. But the *Hartford Business Journal* will continue to prosper by listening carefully to readers, understanding the business marketplace, and delivering a top-quality product.

FOUNDED IN 1992 AS A RESOURCE FOR HANDLING BANKS' CORE PROCESSING requirements, Open Solutions Inc.® quickly became the undisputed leader in the field, which is reflected in revenues that rose a staggering 12,770 percent in five years. In 1999, Open Solutions received the Deloitte Touche/Connecticut Technology Council Fast 50 Award and was ranked number one as the fastest-growing technology

company in the state. The company was also ranked 19th in the nationwide Deloitte Touche Fast 500 program. Explosive growth and change continue today as Open Solutions revolutionizes the industry with on-line banking and e-commerce systems for community banks and credit unions.

Open Solutions succeeds by listening to and understanding the needs of small to mid-size banks and credit unions. The company's founders asked banks and credit unions what they wanted in a core processing system, and their answers led to development of The Complete Banking Solution® and The Complete Credit Union Solution®. These real-time applications support an institution's entire core processing needs, including deposit and loan account processing, customer information, back office, and regulatory requirements.

Introducing Internet Banking and E-Commerce

As Open Solutions—with corporate headquarters located in Glastonbury—continues to offer powerful core processing systems, it is showing banks and credit unions how to leverage the trust they have developed with their customers and members over the years, from their custom-

ers' first savings accounts to their first mortgages. By introducing these institutions to the new world of e-commerce and Internet banking technology, Open Solutions is helping them create community, trust, and value on-line.

Banks and credit unions that participate in the Open Community Network (OCN) provided by Open Solutions can offer a trusted and secure on-line mall with around-the-clock real-time banking services. From the safety of the local financial institution's Internet site, customers can visit the Web sites of nationally known partner suppliers such as Disney Online, Sharper Image, HP Computer, OfficeMax, Hallmark, and Flower.com, and make Internet purchases using a common consolidated shopping cart.

Customers save money by using their bank's on-line network, and banks and credit unions receive a share of retail sales. OCN also gives customers convenient on-line access to their accounts to transfer funds, make balance inquiries, pay bills, and conduct other business. The network even includes a community section, providing regional news and resources, and information about schools, meetings, and events. Two weeks after Open Solutions' new products were announced in Febru-

ary 2000, five institutions—one of which was Savings Bank of Manchester, Connecticut—had already signed up.

"Internet usage doubles every 100 days, and the possibilities are exciting," says Louis Hernandez Jr., Open Solutions chairman and CEO. "We tell banks and credit unions that technology should bring them closer to their customers. Those who identify and market their niche strengths and effectively use information technology will carve themselves a slice of the financial market."

While helping their customers thrive, Open Solutions has effectively managed its own phenomenal growth. By April 2000, Hernandez had raised $20 million from venture capitalists and filed to take the company public. Open Solutions had also added more than 100 employees, bringing its total to 250, and moved into a second building in Glastonbury. The firm continues to expand its presence throughout the United States.

Open Solutions Inc. embraces the challenges of the 21st century as an energetic young company with a powerful vision—to revolutionize the financial industry by offering innovative technology, products, and services.

CLOCKWISE FROM TOP RIGHT: OPEN SOLUTIONS INC. PROVIDES A COMPREHENSIVE SUITE OF PRODUCTS THAT INTEGRATE ELECTRONIC COMMERCE, INTERNET BANKING, AND ENTERPRISE PROCESSING APPLICATIONS FOR SMALL TO MIDSIZE COMMERCIAL BANKS, THRIFTS, AND CREDIT UNIONS.

THE COMPANY'S CORPORATE HEADQUARTERS IS LOCATED IN GLASTONBURY.

OPEN SOLUTIONS' VISION IS TO REVOLUTIONIZE THE FINANCIAL SERVICES SECTOR THROUGH ITS INNOVATIVE TECHNOLOGY PRODUCTS AND SERVICES.

JDS Uniphase Electro-optic Products Division

EVERY TIME SOMEONE LOGS ON TO THE INTERNET, PLACES A PHONE call, or tunes in to cable television, he or she is using technology made possible by JDS Uniphase, a Bloomfield, Connecticut-based entity that is making significant contributions to the growth and success of today's advanced fiber-optic communications networks. JDS Uniphase provides a broad range of fiber-optic components to leading equipment and systems manufacturers in the telecommunications, cable television, and data networking industries.

The company was founded in 1992 as a spin-off of United Technologies Corporation. In 1995, Uniphase Corporation acquired the entrepreneurial group of engineers to expand its market share in telecommunications. As a result of the 1999 merger of Uniphase Corporation and JDS Fitel, Inc., JDS Uniphase now spans the globe with more than 10,000 employees and facilities throughout North America, Europe, and Australia.

The strength of combined capital, a commitment to research and development, and the application of just-in-time manufacturing processes have enabled the company to develop and produce cutting-edge products for the fiber-optic marketplace.

A Leader in Fiber Optics

The JDS Uniphase Electro-optic Products Division (EPD) plays a key role in meeting the needs of communications network providers around the globe. With more than 150,000 square feet of research, design, and production facilities in Bloomfield and Windsor, Connecticut, JDS Uniphase EPD designs and manufactures products that enable electronic data to be transmitted and controlled over fiber-optic networks.

JDS Uniphase EPD products include digital optical modulators that control data flow at rates from 2.5 billion to 40 billion bits per second, and wave-locking devices that keep data within their respective lanes on laser-generated fiber-optic superhighways. Other products include analog modulators for cable television distribution, optical switching devices, and integrated optical subsystems.

"This is an exciting time to be in communications," says Don Bossi, JDS Uniphase EPD's vice president and general manager. "The fiber-optic superhighways are in place and capable of moving massive amounts of data. The challenge is the on-ramps and off-ramps of these information highways. Our products get data on and off quickly, accurately, and reliably so people can use it productively."

A forward-thinking philosophy based on productive partnerships, a passionate commitment to research and development, and a total commitment to customer satisfaction has

STATE-OF-THE-ART WORKSTATIONS ALLOW PRECISE ASSEMBLY OF MICRO-COMPONENTS AT JDS UNIPHASE ELECTRO-OPTIC PRODUCTS DIVISION (LEFT).

ADVANCED CLEAN-ROOM TECHNOLOGY IS EMPLOYED DURING THE MANUFACTURING PROCESS AT JDS UNIPHASE (RIGHT).

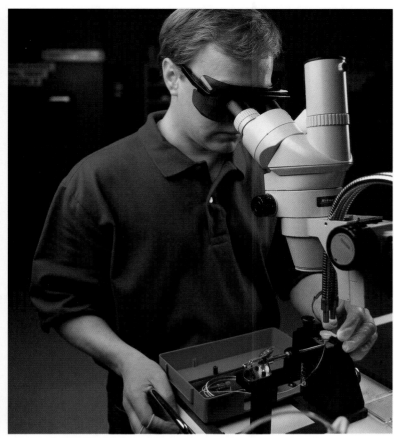

allowed JDS Uniphase to quickly establish and maintain a leadership role in a competitive, rapidly evolving industry.

"We thrive on the evolution of our industry," says Ed Teague, director of technical marketing and business development. "For example, we know that optical frequency control is going to become more important as networks become more complex, so we're investing research and development dollars in products that address these needs."

JDS Uniphase's commitment to research and development is a driving force behind the company's success. The firm invests nearly 10 percent of its annual revenues in research and development, and is thoroughly committed to increasing this investment as the needs of the marketplace change.

"We're helping to build an agile optical network that will allow network providers worldwide to assign dedicated fiber-optic pathways to specific users on demand, in just a matter of hours," says Bossi.

Partnerships Foster Growth

Developing advanced communications technologies requires a considerable investment of time and resources to understand challenges and deliver solutions. The company believes that such customized solu-

tions arise from forging partnerships. "We believe in building long-lasting partnerships with our customers," says Teague. "We work hard to understand the customer's needs now and in the future. We focus on how we can best apply cooperative resources to arrive at the most effective solution."

Bossi sees the partnership philosophy as a dynamic circle made up of JDS Uniphase employees, customers, and vendors. "As a manager, I can stand in the center, stretch out my arms, and 'touch' everyone," he says. "Information moves freely and that stimulates new ideas. It maximizes cooperation and productivity. Everyone benefits."

Sharing ideas and keeping people informed are part of the company's

success formula. "We can retain capable, highly committed team members because we treat our co-workers, our customers, and our community in an open, honest, and ethical manner." says Todd Tucker, vice president of operations. "We deliver results beyond our customers' expectations. We reward innovation and value flexibility as a competitive advantage. We encourage employee development and a balanced lifestyle, and support both the local communities in which we operate and the connected, global community we're helping to build."

The prevailing belief at JDS Uniphase EPD is that everyone is working to improve quality of life on a global scale. "Improving communications is good for society as a whole," Teague says, and Bossi agrees. "It allows people rapid access to information to make informed decisions. It fosters competition—yielding better products and services—and promotes cooperation and growth."

World Citizens

JDS Uniphase sees itself as a world citizen in a growing global community. The company is investing not only in its own growth by expanding its facilities and hiring hundreds of new employees, but also in the future of technology itself through programs in local communities, schools, and colleges. These programs help educators and students alike select and flourish in technical fields related to communications.

JDS Uniphase is helping move information around the globe at the speed of light, helping to build a more powerful and rewarding world for all.

JDS Uniphase's fiber-optic component parts are carefully inspected to ensure optimum quality.

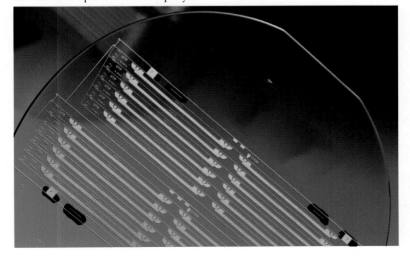

Thin wafers contain electronic data pathways that are incorporated into fiber-optic components made by JDS Uniphase Electro-optic Products Division.

Smith Whiley & Company

MONG INVESTMENT FIRMS, SMITH WHILEY & COMPANY IS UNIQUE. Founder Gwendolyn Smith Iloani's efforts to succeed in Hartford and beyond have helped her create the largest minority- and woman-owned investment advisor and broker dealer firm in New England. Iloani, currently president and CEO of Smith Whiley, opened her first office on

Trumbull Street in 1994.

Smith Whiley is a first for Hartford, but just one of many firsts for Iloani, who has long been on the cutting edge of the investment business. She arrived at Colgate University three years after it went coeducational, and often was the only woman and African-American in her class. She was the first black female hired in the bond investment department at Aetna Inc., and ultimately managed a $9.2 billion portfolio during her tenure there.

Iloani was so successful at Aetna that, when she needed capital to establish her new firm, the company offered to invest, becoming a one-third partner in Smith Whiley. Two years later, Iloani bought out Aetna's share. "Aetna liked the product mix and launched it," says Iloani. "The rest is history."

Iloani's strategy was to create a firm that would offer alternative investment products in diverse private-placement markets—and it has worked. Smith Whiley now has more than $100 million in assets under management. The firm also has an office in Chicago led by Venita Fields, senior managing director. In 1999, *Black Enterprise* magazine listed Smith Whiley as the 12th-largest minority-owned investment manager in the country.

Value Defined, Value Delivered

The firm celebrated its fifth anniversary in 1999, but that was only the beginning. Building on Smith Whiley's tradition of excellence, Iloani hopes to raise assets under management to $1 billion. To achieve this goal, Smith Whiley's investment team will provide asset management and financial services to public and private plan sponsors,

foundations, and endowments. Smith Whiley will also help institutions make alternative investments in venture capital and private equity instead of mainstream investments in stocks, bonds, or mutual funds. The company's clients have included a hospital group, a telecommunications company, insurance companies, and several public pension funds.

To remain successful, Iloani relies on thorough and diligent research, highly specialized skills, and an experienced investment team. Collectively, the principals of Smith Whiley & Company have more than 150 years of institutional investment and consulting experience. They have invested more than $5 billion in alternative investments, including debt and equity private placements, mezzanine debt investments, and targeted investments. The principals have also managed an alternative investment portfolio of more than $11 million for prior employees.

"We seek to blend experience with innovation in designing and managing alternative investment products," says Iloani.

Sound Investments

Smith Whiley's approach to investing is to seek opportunities in underserved sectors, and to balance value and risk, innovation and committed management.

The innovative company also looks closely at unusual deals and finds ways of structuring them to meet the needs of its clients. Since 1999, the firm has invested more than $50 million in businesses as diverse as a North Dakota pig producer and a Florida-based telemedicine Internet provider. Iloani believes that the quality of management is the most important element in the success of an investment, and invests in companies where management has a proven track record and a demonstrated ability to grow the business.

"My job is to identify undervalued opportunities, and then focus on performance and delivery," says Iloani.

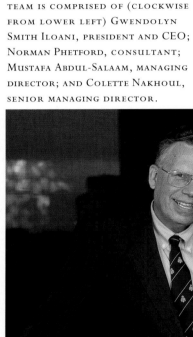

SMITH WHILEY & COMPANY IN HARTFORD IS THE LARGEST WOMAN- AND MINORITY-OWNED INVESTMENT ADVISOR AND BROKER DEALER FIRM IN NEW ENGLAND. THE MANAGEMENT TEAM IS COMPRISED OF (CLOCKWISE FROM LOWER LEFT) GWENDOLYN SMITH ILOANI, PRESIDENT AND CEO; NORMAN PHETFORD, CONSULTANT; MUSTAFA ABDUL-SALAAM, MANAGING DIRECTOR; AND COLETTE NAKHOUL, SENIOR MANAGING DIRECTOR.

{ C B Richard Ellis is the world-market leader in real estate services. Headquartered in Los Angeles, with more than 10,000 employees worldwide, the company serves real estate owners, investors, and occupiers through more than 230 principal offices in 32 countries. ✸ CB Richard Ellis-N.E. Partners, LP is a strategic joint venture formed by CB Richard Ellis and Whittier Partners Group. }

CB Richard Ellis– N. E. Partners, LP

The company's Connecticut headquarters is in Hartford, with nearby offices in Boston, New Haven, and Providence. Its core services portfolio includes property sales, leasing, property management, corporate advisory services, facilities management, mortgage banking, investment management, capital markets, appraisal/valuation, and market research.

The company has the industry's most comprehensive portfolio of products and services. Through these resources and its cumulative expertise, CB Richard Ellis delivers new and innovative real estate solutions every day. Combining brokerage, financial, asset, and corporate advisory services, the company extracts the greatest value for clients from their real estate assets. Clients can expect service and unmatched accountability across geographies, industries, and projects.

Meeting the Challenge

CB Richard Ellis-N.E. Partners, LP realizes that commercial real estate is driven by successful personal and business relationships. By becoming clients' partners, the company's professionals take that notion a step further. Through seamless working relationships and a thorough understanding of customers' objectives, the company can help clients capture greater market opportunities. No

matter how complex a client's needs may be, CB Richard Ellis provides a custom mix of products and services to deliver significant, measurable returns.

Whether providing property owners and investors with comprehensive services, or representing prospective tenants, the company's knowledgeable staff meets the needs of each client. The result is a personalized solution that results in an ongoing professional relationship.

The company's consulting and valuation group is one of the most respected in New England. It has provided numerous valuations on much of the commercial real estate in the Greater Hartford market. Services include valuation analysis, certification, due diligence coordination, and portfolio analysis.

CB Richard Ellis' services extend to property and facilities management, engineering services, and lease administration. The Hartford office alone manages 3.4 million square feet of commercial, industrial, and retail properties and facilities.

To stay current with market conditions, and to make informed judgments, professionals use the latest analytical, marketing, and technological tools. This includes a proprietary database of 40,000 New England tenants, 500 million square feet of property, and 1,500

investors. Researchers collaborate with CB Richard Ellis Torto-Wheaton Research to obtain the national and international econometric forecasts that lead the industry.

As a people-oriented company, CB Richard Ellis strives to be a great place to work. This effort is highlighted by the key employee ownership opportunities of the company's 50/50 local-global joint partnership. The company's caring atmosphere extends into the community, as it regularly and generously contributes time, staff, money, and facilities to various community groups in Hartford and surrounding towns.

With economic, political, and technological factors transforming the world of real estate, CB Richard Ellis-N.E. Partners, LP has the experience, resources, and talent to help clients successfully navigate these changes.

NO MATTER HOW COMPLEX A CLIENT'S NEEDS MAY BE, CB RICHARD ELLIS-N.E. PARTNERS, LP PROVIDES A CUSTOM MIX OF PRODUCTS AND SERVICES TO DELIVER SIGNIFICANT, MEASURABLE RETURNS.

NEW ENGLAND RENAISSANCE   273

Connecticut Children's Medical Center

{ CONNECTICUT CHILDREN'S MEDICAL CENTER HAS DISTINGUISHED ITSELF as a special place dedicated to improving the physical and emotional health of children. More than 145,000 patients visit the center annually for primary care, inpatient admissions, day surgery, emergencies, or specialty clinics. ✸ "With Connecticut Children's Medical Center conveniently located in Hartford," says Larry Gold, president and CEO, }

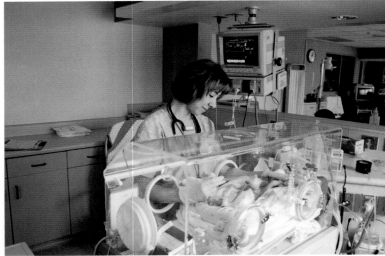

"parents no longer have to go to Boston or New York City to obtain sophisticated medical care for their children. We can manage children with complex health care needs here in Hartford and keep families together."

Full Spectrum of Services

When the 123-bed facility opened in 1996, it consolidated the pediatric personnel and programs that were formerly located at nearby Hartford Hospital, University of Connecticut Health Center, and Newington Children's Hospital into a new, freestanding facility. As a teaching hospital—home of the University of Connecticut School of Medicine residency program in pediatrics—Connecticut Children's is on the leading edge of the latest information and technology.

One of the newest children's hospitals in the United States, Connecticut Children's offers a complete range of pediatric medical and surgical services, including a 24-hour pediatric emergency department staffed by pediatric emergency specialists, as well as a 23-hour medical unit. A neonatal intensive care unit serves critically ill newborns, while the center's 12-bed pediatric intensive care unit serves children with trauma and life-threatening illnesses.

The medical center's pediatric orthopedics service is known worldwide, and its cancer center is involved nationally in research and treatment protocols. The facility also has leading pediatric cardiology services and comprehensive pediatric pulmonary services. Its nationally known gait analysis laboratory is used to diagnose children with walking problems, which can be corrected with surgery.

Caring for Children

Some of the top doctors, researchers, and other professionals in pediatric medicine have been attracted to Connecticut Children's, drawn by an institution that dedicates 100 percent of its resources to children's health. Whether medical students or seasoned professionals, the caring staff understands that children are not little adults: Their medical needs are different, and they do not react to illness or treatments the same ways adults react. For example, many general hospitals use one blood pressure cuff size to fit every patient. But a children's medical center must be able to care for a one-pound premature infant, a 200-pound teenage linebacker, and everyone in between. That's

THE NEONATAL INTENSIVE CARE UNIT AT CONECTICUT CHILDREN'S MEDICAL CENTER SERVES CRITICALLY ILL NEWBORNS, WHILE ITS 12-BED PEDIATRIC INTENSIVE CARE UNIT SERVES CHILDREN WITH TRAUMA AND LIFE-THREATENING ILLNESSES (TOP).

CONNECTICUT CHILDREN'S MEDICAL CENTER—THE STATE'S ONLY FREESTANDING HOSPITAL JUST FOR CHILDREN—HAS WON PRESTIGIOUS NATIONAL ARCHITECTURAL AWARDS FOR ITS INNOVATIVE DESIGN (BOTTOM RIGHT).

CHILD- AND FAMILY-CENTERED CARE IS AT THE HEART OF THE MEDICAL CENTER'S SERVICE TO PATIENTS (BOTTOM LEFT).

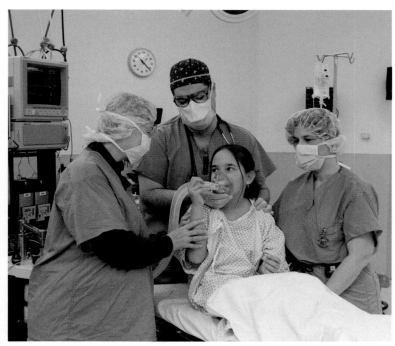

why blood pressure cuffs at the medical center come in 12 sizes, one as small as a Band-Aid.

Likewise, the difference between treating adults and children is dramatically evident during surgery. If an adult loses a pint of blood, it is easily replaced with a transfusion. But if a newborn loses just three to four thimblefuls of blood, the child could die. Consequently, pediatric surgeons at Connecticut Children's use specialized techniques to reduce blood loss during procedures.

Ultimately, caring for children includes understanding their emotional needs, and Connecticut Children's gives special attention to youngsters preparing for surgery. The child life staff prepares children to visit the medical center before admission to learn exactly what will happen, and gives them the opportunity through medical play with anesthesia masks and other equipment to understand what to expect. When possible, youngsters can drive to the operating room in a small Barbie car or jeep, giving them a feeling of control. Once in the operating room, they can choose the scent of roses, pizza, or bubble gum for their anesthesia. Connecticut Children's asks parents to be present in the operating room when their children undergo anesthesia and when they awake after the surgery.

Family-Centered Care

Child- and family-centered care is at the heart of the medical center's service to patients. In

fact, children and families, along with staff, had a hand in designing the hospital. The facility's imaginative, award-winning design includes whimsical geometric forms, playful sculptures, and sparkling glass walls.

Each patient has a private room with windows that open to the outdoors and the hallways. The rooms have private showers and a small sofa bed for parents, who are encouraged to stay overnight. In addition, every floor has well-equipped playrooms where young patients can relax. Intensive care units are private, with large windows to bring in natural light. Private sleep rooms, kitchens, and laundry facilities allow parents to remain close to their children 24 hours a day.

Connecticut Children's Medical Center also supports families' ongoing needs for emotional, educational, and caregiving support. Services include translators to help families communicate in their own languages with medical providers, a library with current information on medical problems and programs, and volunteers who provide respite care.

Serving the Community at Large

The hospital's reach extends beyond its patients and their families and into the Hartford community. With injuries being the leading cause of death and hospitalization for children, Connecticut Children's is a leading advocate for initiatives that protect children from preventable

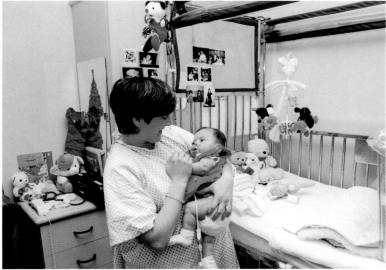

injuries, violence, child abuse, and other physical and emotional trauma. The medical center teams with community agencies and law enforcement to promote education and legislation concerning child safety, such as mandatory bicycle helmets, seat belts, and car seats. Programs assist children in drug-exposed families, help teenagers learn how to resolve problems without violence, and teach parenting skills.

Already, the medical center's influence is extending beyond Hartford to bring medical services closer to children where they live. Through partnerships with community hospitals, the center is sending its specialists on the road to visit children on an outpatient basis around Connecticut.

WITH A HEARTFELT BELIEF THAT "KIDS ARE GREAT, WE JUST MAKE 'EM BETTER," CONNECTICUT CHILDREN'S MEDICAL CENTER IS FULLY COMMITTED TO IMPROVING THE HEALTH OF CHILDREN THROUGH LEADERSHIP IN SERVICE, EDUCATION, AND RESEARCH.

OEM of Connecticut, Inc.

T O BE SUCCESSFUL, SMALL-BUSINESS OWNERS MUST FOCUS ON STRATEGIC planning, revenue, and other business matters. They also must manage employer issues that are costly distractions, such as payroll taxes, unemployment insurance and workers' compensation claims, medical benefits, labor laws, and government compliance. Outsourcing Employment Management (OEM) of Connecticut, Inc. takes care

of those issues, giving small-business people the time needed to run their businesses.

OEM is a professional employer organization (PEO), a relatively new type of business. As a PEO, OEM enters into contracts with small to midsize businesses to establish and maintain employer relationships with the workers assigned to the businesses' clients. As a co-employer, OEM assumes substantial employer rights, responsibilities, and risks, and pays and reports wages and employment taxes out of its own accounts. The business owner simply writes one check per pay period to cover payroll, taxes, benefits, and administration, while OEM does the rest. The arrangement frees business owners to focus their own resources, time, and energy on increasing their bottom line.

CEO David Fernandez, who founded OEM in 1996, says, "OEM and other PEOs save our clients time, cut their overhead, give their employees better benefits, and help reduce turnover. They can concentrate on their business without the challenges and distractions associated with the business of employment."

OEM's clients include bakeries, tire stores, Internet companies, manufacturers, and construction companies with an average of 40

to 50 employees. Based in East Hartford, the company has branches in Pennsylvania and Atlanta, and belongs to the National Association of Professional Employer Organizations. Together, OEM's key business associates have more than 25 years of experience in the insurance field.

Win, Win, Win

OEM can supply small businesses with five critical functions: human resources, workers' compensation,

employee benefits, payroll administration, and organizational assistance. This arrangement benefits the business, its employees, and the government.

For the business owner, OEM provides professional compliance and claims management for workers' compensation and unemployment insurance—saving the client a high volume of paperwork hassles. OEM also can provide screening, training, employee handbooks, personnel forms, policies and procedures, performance appraisal assistance, and similar services.

The savings in time and money for OEM's clients are considerable. The U.S. Small Business Administration says the average small-business owner spends up to 25 percent of his or her time handling employee-related paperwork. In addition, the average annual cost of regulation, paperwork, and tax compliance for firms with fewer than 500 employees is about $5,000 per employee, compared with $3,400 per employee for firms with more than 500 employees.

Until the advent of PEOs, small companies had been hard pressed to offer their employees the competitive

OEM OF CONNECTICUT, INC. SUPPLIES SMALL BUSINESSES WITH FIVE CRITICAL FUNCTIONS—HUMAN RESOURCES, WORKERS' COMPENSATION, EMPLOYEE BENEFITS, PAYROLL ADMINISTRATION, AND ORGANIZATIONAL ASSISTANCE—BENEFITING THE BUSINESS, ITS EMPLOYEES AND THE GOVERNMENT.

medical, disability, and life insurance benefits, as well as 401(k) plans, that are typical benefits at larger organizations. Due to economies of scale, OEM has tremendous purchasing power, which the firm uses to offer these plans to its clients at affordable costs. Small-business owners can then attract and retain top employees. Besides offering purchasing services, OEM can administer a client company's benefits, enroll its employees, and manage its benefits program. The company can also provide clients with credit unions, prescription care, and other extras for their employees.

Besides being able to obtain benefits that previously were unavailable to them, employees of OEM's clients receive professional orientation and employee handbooks, improved employer/employee communications, and up-to-date information on labor regulations, workers' rights, and work site safety. Professional assistance with employment-related problems is available as well. And, most important, their paychecks are distributed accurately and on time.

OEM can also provide and administer workers' compensation insurance, help manage safety requirements and claims that may occur, and reduce the risks associated with being in business. The government benefits from the arrangement

since OEM consolidates several small companies' employment tax filings into one, provides professional preparation and reporting, and facilitates accelerated collection of taxes.

A Growth Industry

With the explosion of new Internet businesses, the number of small businesses is growing at an unprecedented rate across the country. For example, there were more than 7,100 Internet service providers in 2000,

up 41 percent over the previous year. Most of these businesses have fewer than 12 employees.

As a direct result of new small-business growth, OEM and other PEOs are experiencing 30 percent growth each year. Also, the total number of PEOs themselves is increasing—from 250 in 1987 to about 2,500 in 2000.

Several factors are driving the growth of the PEO industry. Since 1980, there has been a significant increase in employment-related federal, state, and local laws and regulations, and the entrepreneurs who started small to midsize businesses no longer have the expertise to manage all aspects of their businesses. Few can afford to hire a full-time staff—an accountant, a human resources professional, a lawyer, a risk manager, a benefits manager, and a manager of information services—to handle the business of employment. At the same time, today's American workers demand quality employee benefits at affordable prices.

"Having been in the insurance business, I know that a business owner might have to talk to two or three brokers every year, and repeat that for every line of benefits he or she wants to offer," says Fernandez. "It's a tremendous loss of time and energy. OEM offers one-stop shopping. OEM is a real service business. We bring benefits to people who have never had them, and, bottom line, we help make small companies extraordinarily successful."

WORKING WITH THE TEAM OF PROFESSIONALS AT OEM FREES BUSINESS OWNERS TO FOCUS THEIR OWN RESOURCES, TIME, AND ENERGY ON INCREASING THEIR BOTTOM LINE.

Permatex, Inc.

THE NAME PERMATEX HAS BEEN SYNONYMOUS WITH QUALITY AND dependability in the motor vehicle maintenance and repair industry for more than 90 years. From its humble beginnings in 1909 as a manufacturer of shellac to bind bicycle tires to rims, Permatex, Inc. has grown into a multinational leader in the automotive specialty chemical products market. ❋ "Permatex products have helped

keep motor vehicles on the road for nearly as long as the public has been driving," says Pat Formica, company president. He explains that Permatex is a leader in chemical gaskets, a market the firm created in 1915 and continued to improve upon through the years. "Gasket failure was a major problem in early automobiles," Formica says. "Permatex came up with a solution, and has been an innovator ever since. Our products help professional automotive technicians and serious do-it-yourselfers repair cars in a way that minimizes the chances that a problem will reoccur."

In addition to chemical gaskets and related products, this Hartford-based company is a market share leader in anaerobic thread lockers; adhesives and superglues; silicones; and hand cleaners. Permatex also enjoys a leading position in tire care products.

Permatex began a new chapter in its history during 1999, when it severed ties with an industrial corpora-

tion that had owned the business for 27 years, and became an independent company. The new Permatex is aggressively building on its reputation for high-quality products and excellent service. The company is applying its expertise in research and technology to explore a variety of potential and existing markets, including automotive, heavy duty, power sports, aviation, marine, home and garden, and retail.

A Bright Future

Permatex has developed a strategic plan for the 21st century to achieve challenging growth goals. Its formula for success emphasizes providing customers with high-quality products and services, and powerful brand names. The company plans to leverage its most recognized products under the Permatex®, Right Stuff®, and Fast Orange® brand names by expanding current product lines and introducing additional products. In 1999 and 2000

alone, the firm introduced more than 30 new products, including a promising line of functional fluids such as Permatex Fuel Injector and Carburetor Cleaner and Permatex Super Heavy Duty Brake Fluid.

In addition to its powerful brand names, the company is taking advantage of its sales and distribution organization—one of the strongest in the country—and the top-notch manufacturing processes and technologies that have become a Permatex hallmark.

To fulfill its goal of becoming an industry giant, Permatex plans to grow through strategic acquisitions of complementary businesses, products, and brands. In 2000, the company acquired No Touch North America, a market leader in tire and wheel care whose patented formula for a one-step tire care product revolutionized the category in 1991.

Outstanding employees are key drivers to the company's success as

AT THE HELM OF PERMATEX, INC. IS PAT FORMICA (LEFT), PRESIDENT. PAM BRUNELLE (RIGHT) IS THE MANAGER OF COMPENSATION AND HUMAN RESOURCES INFORMATION SYSTEMS.

PERMATEX PRODUCTS HAVE BEEN PROVEN EFFECTIVE ON THE RACE-TRACK AND ARE TRUSTED BY AUTOMOTIVE PROFESSIONALS THROUGHOUT THE WORLD. AMONG THEM IS BILL VENTURINI JR., DRIVER OF A PERMATEX-SPONSORED AUTOMOBILE RACING CLUB OF AMERICA (ARCA) RACE CAR.

well. "Our employees are the cream of the automotive aftermarket crop," says Formica. "With rapid growth around the next turn, we continue to attract top talent from the automotive and chemicals industries."

Taking Care of Valued Customers

Permatex has an unwavering focus on customers, who run the gamut from enthusiastic do-it-yourselfers to professional automotive technicians. Formica says, "Our goal is to continuously exceed our customers' expectations of us. Simply put, they are the judges of the quality of our products and their satisfaction ultimately determines our success."

Customer and end-user education and training are the centerpiece of Permatex's marketing strategy. The company provides free product training clinics attended by several thousand automotive technicians, installers, and vocational-technical students each year. These clinics teach people in the automotive repair industry how Permatex products can help them save time, reduce costs, and increase repair reliability. They learn the proper use of products, repair procedures, and best practices, and receive informative reference materials and free samples.

The clinics have been wildly successful since their introduction in 1999. Permatex has set a goal of reaching 100,000 automotive repair professionals per year through this unique educational venue.

From its Hartford headquarters, Permatex directs a growing global automotive aftermarket enterprise

serving North America, the Pacific Rim, South America, Europe, and Africa. "Our manufacturing plants, distribution centers, and offices are strategically located to help us achieve our growth goals," says Formica.

Formica sees great opportunities ahead for both the company and its employees. "There is a tremendous entrepreneurial spirit within the new Permatex," he says. "From our per-

spective, the road ahead is wide open to us to build this company into a world-class business. We will accomplish this by leveraging the deep strengths of our employees, brands, and distribution system to acquire and quickly assimilate complementary businesses, to develop and introduce new products, and to discover or create new markets for our products."

PERMATEX FAST ORANGE® HAND CLEANER IS PACKAGED IN THE COMPANY'S STATE-OF-THE-ART SOLON, OHIO, MANUFACTURING, DISTRIBUTION, AND TECHNICAL CENTER.

Towery Publishing, Inc.

In all its endeavors, this Memphis-based company strives to be synonymous with service, utility, and quality.

A Diversity of Community-Based Products

Over the years, Towery has become the largest producer of published materials for North American chambers of commerce. From membership directories that enhance business-to-business communication to visitor and relocation guides tailored to reflect the unique qualities of the communities they cover, the company's chamber-oriented materials offer comprehensive information on dozens of topics, including housing, education, leisure activities,

health care, and local government.

In 1998, the company acquired Cincinnati-based Target Marketing, an established provider of detailed city street maps to more than 200 chambers of commerce throughout the United States and Canada. Now a division of Towery, Target offers full-color maps that include local landmarks and points of interest, such as recreational parks, shopping centers, golf courses, schools, industrial parks, city and county limits, subdivision names, public buildings, and even block numbers on most streets.

In 1990, Towery launched the Urban Tapestry Series, an award-winning collection of oversized, hardbound photojournals detailing

the people, history, culture, environment, and commerce of various metropolitan areas. These coffee-table books highlight a community through three basic elements: an introductory essay by a noted local individual, an exquisite collection of four-color photographs, and profiles of the companies and organizations that animate the area's business life.

To date, more than 80 Urban Tapestry Series editions have been published in cities around the world, from New York to Vancouver to Sydney. Authors of the books' introductory essays include former U.S. President Gerald Ford (Grand Rapids), former Alberta Premier Peter Lougheed (Calgary), CBS anchor Dan Rather (Austin), ABC anchor Hugh Downs (Phoenix), best-selling mystery author Robert B. Parker (Boston), American Movie Classics host Nick Clooney (Cincinnati), Senator Richard Lugar (Indianapolis), and Challenger Center founder June Scobee Rodgers (Chattanooga).

To maintain hands-on quality in all of its periodicals and books, Towery has long used the latest production methods available. The company was the first production environment in the United States to combine desktop publishing with color separations and image scanning to produce finished film suitable for burning plates for four-color printing. Today, Towery relies on state-of-the-art digital prepress services to produce more than 8,000 pages each year, containing well over 30,000 high-quality color images.

An Internet Pioneer

By combining its long-standing expertise in community-oriented published materials with advanced production capabilities, a global sales force, and extensive data management capabilities, Towery has emerged as a significant provider of Internet-based city information. In keeping with its overall focus on

community resources, the company's Internet efforts represent a natural step in the evolution of the business.

The primary product lines within the Internet division are the introCity™ sites. Towery's intro-City sites introduce newcomers, visitors, and longtime residents to every facet of a particular community, while simultaneously placing the local chamber of commerce at the forefront of the city's Internet activity. The sites include newcomer information, calendars, photos, citywide business listings with everything from nightlife to shopping to family fun, and on-line maps

pinpointing the exact location of businesses, schools, attractions, and much more.

Decades of Publishing Expertise

In 1972, current President and CEO J. Robert Towery succeeded his parents in managing the printing and publishing business they had founded nearly four decades earlier. Soon thereafter, he expanded the scope of the company's published materials to include *Memphis* magazine and other successful regional and national publications. In 1985, after selling its locally focused assets, Towery began the trajectory on

which it continues today, creating community-oriented materials that are often produced in conjunction with chambers of commerce and other business organizations.

Despite the decades of change, Towery himself follows a long-standing family philosophy of unmatched service and unflinching quality. That approach extends throughout the entire organization to include more than 120 employees at the Memphis headquarters, another 80 located in Northern Kentucky outside Cincinnati, and more than 40 sales, marketing, and editorial staff traveling to and working in a growing list of client cities. All of its products, and more information about the company, are featured on the Internet at www.towery.com.

In summing up his company's steady growth, Towery restates the essential formula that has driven the business since its first pages were published: "The creative energies of our staff drive us toward innovation and invention. Our people make the highest possible demands on themselves, so I know that our future is secure if the ingredients for success remain a focus on service and quality."

TOWERY PUBLISHING WAS THE FIRST PRODUCTION ENVIRONMENT IN THE UNITED STATES TO COMBINE DESKTOP PUBLISHING WITH COLOR SEPARATIONS AND IMAGE SCANNING TO PRODUCE FINISHED FILM SUITABLE FOR BURNING PLATES FOR FOUR-COLOR PRINTING. TODAY, THE COMPANY'S STATE-OF-THE-ART NETWORK OF MACINTOSH AND WINDOWS WORKSTATIONS ALLOWS IT TO PRODUCE MORE THAN 8,000 PAGES EACH YEAR, CONTAINING MORE THAN 30,000 HIGH-QUALITY COLOR IMAGES (ABOVE).

THE TOWERY FAMILY'S PUBLISHING ROOTS CAN BE TRACED TO 1935, WHEN R.W. TOWERY (FAR LEFT) BEGAN PRODUCING A SERIES OF COMMUNITY HISTORIES IN TENNESSEE, MISSISSIPPI, AND TEXAS. THROUGHOUT THE COMPANY'S HISTORY, THE FOUNDING FAMILY HAS CONSISTENTLY EXHIBITED A COMMITMENT TO CLARITY, PRECISION, INNOVATION, AND VISION (LEFT).

{Cataloging-in-Publication Data}

Hartford—New England renaissance / introduction by Bob Steele ; art direction by Enrique Espinosa

    p. cm. — (Urban tapestry series)

  Includes index.

   ISBN 1-881096-83-1 (alk. paper)

    1. Hartford (Conn.)—Civilization. 2. Hartford (Conn.)—Pictorial works. 3. Hartford (Conn.)—Economic conditions. 4. Business enterprises—Connecticut—Hartford. I. Steele, Bob, 1911- II. Series.

F104.H3 H36 2000

974.6'3—dc21

00-53632

Publisher: J. Robert Towery **Executive Publisher**: Jenny McDowell **National Sales Manager**: Stephen Hung **Marketing Director**: Carol Culpepper **Project Director**: Mary Whelan **Executive Editor**: David B. Dawson **Managing Editor**: Lynn Conlee **Senior Editors**: Carlisle Hacker, Brian L. Johnston **Editors**: Jay Adkins, Stephen M. Deusner, Danna M. Greenfield, Sabrina Schroeder **Editor/Caption Writer**: Rebecca E. Farabough **Editor/Profile Manager**: Ginny Reeves **Profile Writer**: Deena C. Williams **Creative Director**: Brian Groppe **Photography Editor**: Jonathan Postal **Photographic Consultant**: Toni Finch Kellar **Profile Designers**: Rebekah Barnhardt, Laurie Beck, Glen Marshall **Production Manager**: Brenda Pattat **Photography Coordinator**: Robin Lankford **Production Assistants**: Robert Barnett, Loretta Lane, Robert Parrish **Digital Color Supervisor**: Darin Ipema **Digital Color Technicians**: Eric Friedl, Brent Salazar, Mark Svetz **Digital Scanning Technicians**: Zac Ives, Brad Long **Production Resources Manager**: Dave Dunlap Jr. **Print Coordinator**: Beverly Timmons

Towery Publishing, Inc.

The Towery Building

1835 Union Avenue

Memphis, TN 38104

WWW.TOWERY.COM

PRINTED IN CHINA

{Photographers}

Based in Durham, North Carolina, **Bruce R. Feeley** is a freelance editorial photographer and has been the principal photographer for the American Dance Festival since 1994. His clients include the *New York Times*, the American Dance Festival, and *Sports Illustrated*. His most recent work has been in the field of travel photography, focusing on the U.S. East Coast.

Born in Boston, **Jonathan Halberg** has lived in Ohio, California, and Alabama. Halberg specializes in advertising, fashion, and sports photography.

Hillstrom Stock Photo, established in 1967, is a full-service stock photography agency based in Chicago. Its largest files consist of architecture, agricultural background, classic auto, garden, and high-risk adventure/sports images.

Bud Lee studied at the Columbia University School of Fine Arts in New York and the National Academy of Fine Arts. A self-employed photojournalist, he founded the Florida Photographers Workshop and the Iowa Photographers Workshop. Lee's work can be seen in *Esquire, Life, Travel & Leisure, Rolling Stone*, the *Washington Post*, and *New York Times*, as well as in numerous Urban Tapestry Series publications.

After studying art in his native Ireland, **James Lemass** moved to Cambridge, Massachusetts, in 1987. His specialties include people and travel photography, and his photographs have appeared in several other Towery publications.

Lanny Nagler is a Hartford-based commercial photographer specializing in corporate-industrial, advertising, and travel photography. He has been the recipient of numerous awards from organizations including the Connecticut Art Directors Club and the Art Directors Club of New York. Nagler is on the Board of Directors of the Connecticut Chapter of the American Society of Media Photographers.

A resident of rural Scotland, Connecticut, **Leslie M. Newman** portrays the people, scenes, lifestyles, and activities of her native New England. She has had work published in *Sierra Club Outings, National Gardening*, and the *Fairfield County Advocate*, and is a member of the North American Nature Photography Association.

As a student, **Karen O'Maxfield** had her work accepted to the prestigious Maine Photo Workshop exhibit in New York City. Returning to her native West Hartford in 1985, she founded her own business, Studio O'Maxfield, which specializes in fine-art stock photography and graphic design services.

Photophile, established in San Diego in 1967, has in excess of 1 million color images in stock, culled from more than 85 contributing local and international photographers. Subjects range from images of Southern California to adventure sports, wildlife and underwater scenes, business, industry, people, science and research, health and medicine, and travel photography. Included on Photophile's client list are American Express, *Guest Informant*, Franklin Stoorza, and Princess Cruises.

A professional stock photographer for more than 25 years, **Vincent Salvatore** specializes in landscape, nature, and historical photography. His work has been published in books, magazines, calendars, cards, and brochures, and is also part of a corporate collection.

Specializing in jazz, period architecture, and designs of nature photography, **William J. Shea** provided the cover photo for Claudio Roditi's *The Book of Articulations*. He is the city photographer for Manchester, Connecticut, and has contributed to the Christmas in April program.

Once serving as studio manager for Michele Clement, **Darcey Stone** now owns Darcey Stone Photography and specializes in commercial photography, advertising, and graphic design. Her favorite subjects are landscape and portrait photography.

Other contributing organizations include the Connecticut Historical Society. For information on photographers with images appearing in *Hartford: New England Renaissance*, please contact Towery Publishing.

{Index of Profiles}